The
BASSET HOUND

EDITED BY
COLIN AND TRISH WELLS

BEST of
BREED

ACKNOWLEDGEMENTS

The publishers would like to thank the following for help with photography: Mike Doolan, Patience Waldren (Nedlaw), Colin and Trish Wells (Kortebin), Sandra Allen (Fivevalleys), Tina Watkins (Blackvein), Sally Goodall, Pets As Therapy. Special thanks are due to Sue Danel, and members of the South West Branch of the Basset Hound Club, for extra help with photography.

Cover photo: © Tracy Morgan Animal Photography (www.animalphotographer.co.uk)
Dog featured is Brackenacre Gorgeous, owned by Mrs C Allchorne.

Page 38 © Sabine Stuewer – Tierfoto (www.stuewer-tierfoto.de)

The British Breed Standard reproduced in Chapter 7 is the copyright of the Kennel Club and published with the Club's kind permission. Extracts from the American Breed Standard are reproduced by kind permission of the American Kennel Club.

THE QUESTION OF GENDER
**The 'he' pronoun is used throughout this book instead of the rather impersonal 'it',
but no gender bias is intended.**

First published in 2012 by The Pet Book Publishing Company Limited
Chepstow, NP16 7LG. UK

ISBN
978-1-906305-54-3
1-906305-54-4

Printed and bound in China through Printworks Int. Ltd.

CONTENTS

GETTING TO KNOW BASSET HOUNDS

Chapter 1

The Basset Hound is quite a big dog; he should not be considered small just because he has short legs. As an achondroplastic breed the Basset has a normal-sized body and head but is severely foreshortened in the legs. Other achondroplastic breeds are the Dachshund, the Skye Terrier, the Dandie Dinmont, and the Welsh Corgi. It is an inheritable genetic condition that affects only the development of the long limbs. The growth is arrested, due to abnormal development of the cartilage at the ends of the long bones, resulting in congenital dwarfism. However, the stunted bones, which are frequently bowed, have far greater strength than 'normal' legs, provided there are no growth injuries. Humans may also carry the gene for achondroplasia.

HUNTING DOGS

The various Kennel Clubs throughout the world classify dogs as 'Sporting' breeds and 'Non-sporting' breeds. Historically, dogs were used mainly as guards or hunters. Apart from the necessity of putting meat on the table, the nobility regarded hunting as a major pastime – a 'sport'. Consequently, throughout the world, the basic premise has been: "Is the dog suitable to be used for hunting (or 'sporting') purposes or not?"

Within this simple classification, various breeds are grouped together by their function. In the non-sporting breeds, there are the working dogs, such as the St. Bernard and the Mastiff, and the pastoral breeds, such as the Border Collie and the Old English Sheepdog. The sporting breeds are also divided by their use. For example, dogs that can go to

ground to hunt are basically named as terriers (from 'terre', the French word for 'earth'); Gundogs include the breeds that are used specifically to flush game to the gun, or collectors of game that have fallen to the gun. Hounds are subdivided into sighthounds, such as the Greyhound or Whippet, who chase and catch the 'game', and scenthounds that follow a scent until they tire the prey sufficiently to catch and dispatch it. The Basset Hound, the Bloodhound and the Beagle are included in this subdivision.

A LAYMAN'S DESCRIPTION

If you ask what a Basset Hound looks like, most people will answer, "Ah! Fred Basset! He's the one with long ears and short legs who chases rabbits." Many will add that they are "sad-looking dogs with long bodies and short legs. They are brown and white and have long ears". Those who have personal experience of the breed will tell you that they are "full of character, independent, and have a mind of their own – just like Fred Basset."

Fred Basset, the cartoon character devised by Alex Graham, first appeared in London's *Daily Mail* on 8 July 1964. This was syndicated around the world, and he went on to feature in the *Chicago Tribune*. There is no doubt that Fred Basset put the breed on the world map.

WHY DOES A BASSET LOOK THE WAY HE DOES?

In the early days of 'formal' hunting (c. 7th century), the original working function of larger-bodied dogs with very short legs was to enter the sets and dens of quarry, such as fox and badger. Small dogs, while bold and courageous, would be no match for such animals, who would fight back. The Basset's short, hard and non-curly coat does not pick up debris – and the skin is supple

THE BASSET NOSE

All dogs have a keen sense of smell and this is the first of the senses to develop in a newborn puppy. When the mother leaves the puppies for a short while, they will crawl to the area of the puppy box where the scent of the mother is the strongest.

When we refer to the 'nose' of a hound, it is a reference to the scenting ability - the ability to pick up the smallest molecule of scent possible. It is, in fact, the olfactory nerves at the back of the nose that are significant, as they transfer the scent to the brain, although it is considered that the muzzle – particularly the length of muzzle – plays an important part in determining the scenting ability in a breed.

It is most important that the nostrils are large and open so that they can receive the scent. Bassets have the ability, as do most mammals, to flair their nostrils in order to take in as much of the scent as possible. What particularly helps the Basset to 'move' the scent towards his nostrils are his long ears and slightly loose skin, which will cause the

warm, moist breath of the dog to stir the scent particles and 'lift' them towards the nose.

The tail is also an indicator that the Basset has 'found' a scent – it will be held straight up, sabre fashion, and it will appear that only the tip is wagging frenziedly in the air. A white tip to the tail is an important requirement of the huntsman so that he can see the Basset if he is hunting in deep undergrowth.

Hugh B.C. Pollard, author of The Mystery of Scent (Eyre & Spottiswood 1937), gives a scientific explanation of how the prey animal's scent molecules settle on the ground, spreading out in a thin film (like a little drop of petrol on water). In slightly moist conditions, the scent molecules will lift and rise into the air 'on the back' of the water molecules. The greater the amount of water vapour molecules evaporating into the air, the more scent molecules can be lifted. Obviously too many water vapour molecules (as in fog) spreads the scent too thinly and it cannot be easily traced.

Comparing the Bloodhound (right) and the Basset (below), we can see that the Basset has the proportions of a large dog but with short legs.

enough to stretch if it catches on a protruding root. This means a dog can wriggle backwards in order to free himself, and can then go forwards again without having torn his skin. The loose skin on his head and neck will 'give' and protect the eyes and the neck against the bite of cornered prey. The long ears would also give some protection to the face and the ear canal itself.

Later, with the invention of guns, it was found that the attributes that made the Basset types ideal for flushing (or killing) quarry from its den was also ideal for finding and 'flushing' game from the dense thickets in the forests. The Basset was short enough to go under the majority of the undergrowth – and the skin was loose and supple enough not to tear badly if it was caught in the briars. The colours of pale and dark tan and black, and variations of markings of the coat, blended with the vegetation, so the Basset would move the game gently and slowly towards the guns without frightening it.

TEMPERAMENT

Basset Hounds take everything in their stride and, when care has been taken with their breeding, they are an affable, placid breed that is also very affectionate.

The Basset has an enormous capacity for fun, but he hates to be laughed at unless he has made a joke. Once a Basset finds a 'joke' that makes you laugh, he will trot it out on a regular basis so that you can laugh together – for the rest of his life! He does not like being seriously teased – neither does any human – but he will enjoy a relatively short game of 'tease' provided he is then given the object of his desire. A Basset Hound is intelligent enough to tease you on occasion. He may steal your slipper and then bring it back, only to take it away again as you reach for it. This will be repeated a few times before the slipper is surrendered. All the time the Basset will be wagging his tail in delight and you may probably hear a muted "uff uff" noise, almost like a laugh.

If you are absorbed in your book or newspaper, a quiet "umf" at your side will tell you that your Basset is ready for some attention and play. Ignore the respectful "umf" and your book or newspaper may suddenly be replaced by a Basset head, with twinkling eyes, asking for a game, or a cuddle – either will suit him!

Bitches tend to become rather more serious as they reach two to three years old – but like many an old grandmother, an older bitch will be happy, figuratively speaking, to lift up her skirts and romp with a child or an adult.

Dogs tend to remain 'big, daft lads' until they are around seven years old. A older male will then become more staid and, rather than chase a ball, he will be like an old great-grandfather, preferring the comfort of his old chair near the fire – but he will play if you really insist.

On the whole, the majority of well-bred and carefully reared Basset Hounds are of good temperament and remain so – provided that they are treated sensibly. However, an unpleasant or frightening situation as a puppy may leave a bad impression.

VOCAL BASSETS

Like a child, a Basset can be noisy when playing – and, like a child – when he goes quiet he is either asleep or up to mischief! However, even when asleep, a Basset is not necessarily quiet; they snore – quite loudly at times.

A Basset can certainly be noisy, but he is not a true guard dog. He will object to the neighbours across the boundary fence, but will greet them like long-lost friends when they meet face to face. Conversely, he will sit at the gate, watching the workmen across the street, without making a sound.

The sounds a Basset makes can be quite varied, from the very quiet "umph" (which gradually gets more insistent and a little louder in order to attract your attention) to a loud yodel when playing and chasing and laughing and jumping and shouting with others. The yodel can sometimes be heard if a Basset 'puts up' a rabbit and chases it, or finds and

Nose down and tail up – a Basset has thoughts for nothing else when he is on a scent trail.

starts to follow a very fresh and interesting scent.

Bassets are not 'yappy' dogs. The bark of a Basset Hound could be described as "deep down, brown and velvety". It is rarely shrill, though in Bassets that have been neutered too early it can remain somewhat higher pitched.

If you are the type to 'chatter away' to your Basset Hound, some will 'talk' and tell you such a tale with an "arwu, umph, arwar, uhh" – and they will be perfectly happy with any reply you make, such as, "Did you really? Well, fancy that!"

Occasionally a fast-asleep Basset will start to twitch as he is dreaming and then wake himself up with a "yip yip" and a howl that starts deep in his belly; he will then look at you accusingly as if *you* have made this awful noise to wake him up!

A sad and lonely Basset can howl – and, oh, can he howl! It starts with a low "arr", climbs to a loud and long, higher-pitched "ruuu", and then "ruu ruu ruu", with repeats of "arruuu ruu ruu" over and over again. It is not a noise that the neighbours relish.

If your Basset is left alone and has the run of the house, he may start to feel bored and lonely. He might amuse himself by finding 'toys', such as a cushion, and then disembowelling it, or a table leg and then chewing it. But when boredom sets in, he will feel sad and is quite likely to start to howl. However, a Basset who is used to being in a crate will go to sleep, and will rest undisturbed until you return.

TRAINABILITY

The Basset Hound is, firstly, a sporting breed; he belongs in the Hound group, and is classed as a scenthound. Historically, scenthounds have led humans in the hunt. People followed *them*. Many Bassets, if not firmly controlled, still believe that we should continue to 'follow' them, and that we should understand and accept that they are far superior to ourselves.

A child who is indulged and spoilt is not a nice person. An adult Basset who has been indulged and spoilt as a puppy is not only a 'not-nice person' – but could become a menace as they seek to impose their will on their human family, or, even worse and more dangerously, on non-family members.

This is a thinking breed. A Basset Hound is a dog who can work things out to his own advantage; he can be trained, but only by agreement. Never leave unattended food on a table near a Basset Hound – not even a fruit bowl. Where food is concerned he is the ultimate opportunist thief and, despite his low stature, he can easily reach up to steal things from a kitchen work-surface. Ideally, there should be a closed door – or a gate – between a Basset Hound and the kitchen.

When scolded for being naughty, a Basset will assume a particularly sad demeanour. In this situation, it is best for

humans to make sure they have the last word, then turn away and avoid eye contact with another human. If a Basset sees you smile, he will know that he has escaped censure and he will decide that his misdeed is worth trying again!

LIFE EXPECTANCY

A fit and healthy Basset Hound can be quite long-lived. Many dogs reach double figures, a number live into their mid-teens – and I know of one who celebrated a 17th birthday!

A Basset will howl if he is bored or lonely.

LIVING WITH OTHER DOGS

A Basset Hound is, essentially, a sociable pack animal in exactly the same way as any member of a wolf pack. He will see you and your children as part of his pack; if you have another dog – no matter what breed – he or she will be counted as a part of the pack.

A Basset does not need any other company apart from his pack, though he will enjoy other company in the same way that we enjoy the occasional social company of our friends. Out on his daily walk, a Basset Hound will affably meet and greet his canine friends old and new – but the greeting with another Basset Hound is subtly different. They appear more relaxed as if they find it easy to 'read' each other, and when a Basset meets another Basset who is a particular friend they will nudge and sniff under each other's ears in greeting.

OTHER ANIMALS

A Basset Hound will quite happily live with a cat, provided the cat is happy to live with the Basset Hound; if the cat will allow it, they may become best friends. If you have a cat who gets on with your Basset, it will be counted as a part of the pack; if you have a cat who remains aloof, it will be counted as being attached to the pack, though not a part of it.

Care must be taken if you plan to keep a Basset alongside small caged pets, such as hamsters and gerbils – but this applies equally to all breeds of dog. Initial introductions must be supervised, and it would be unwise to leave a Basset in a room unattended, even when such a pet is in its cage – he might want to 'help' it out of the cage in order to play. Obviously, you would never allow a small pet to run free in the presence of a Basset – remember, he is a hunting dog and instinct may well take over.

A young Basset bitch has been known to live sociably – and safely – with a very large pet house-rabbit, although the rabbit was bigger than the puppy when she first joined the family at eight weeks old.

GETTING ON WITH CHILDREN

Because of their built-in affability, a well-bred Basset Hound can be an ideal companion for a child of any age. However, it would be unwise to allow unsupervised playing with a very young child, as an exuberant, fully grown Basset can easily knock a young child over.

Sometimes it is the Basset Hound who is at risk from an older child, who may tease him to the point of frustration, which could result in the child being bitten. It must always be appreciated that the temperament of a Hound is different to that of a Gundog or a Toy breed. Hounds were bred to think for themselves – to go out and hunt with man following him, or to work

The kindly Basset is an ideal companion for children, as long as mutual respect is established.

independently, as were many of the terriers and guarding breeds. Bassets are not normally aggressive, but they do have a strong sense of place within the pack and consider that any place has to be earned. Pack members – and this includes children – who abuse their position may have to be reminded. Teasing is a form of bullying; a strongwilled child who is bullied in the playground is more likely to punch or kick back at the bully than allow himself to be pushed into a lower place within the playground pack. The same holds true when a Basset is bullied or teased.

A NEW BABY?

If you own a Basset, and then start a family, you must make preparations so that the new arrival is happily accepted as a member of the 'pack'.

Dogs do recognise pregnancy and may become very protective of the soon-to-be mother. When the baby is brought home, let the Basset, under careful supervision, see and smell it properly. Talk to your Basset and give him a fuss so that he understands he is not being excluded, but he must be careful around the new arrival. Try to get into the habit of talking to the Basset and the baby together whilst attending to the baby, and vice versa. In this way the dog feels part of what is going on – and the child soon learns to talk!

However, as with any other breed of dog, it would be unwise to leave very young babies and toddlers alone with a Basset Hound – particularly for the dog's

A Basset loves to be included in family activities.

safety as far as some toddlers are concerned. Our daughter missed out on the crawling stage; she walked by 10 months, having learned by clinging to a helpful Basset Hound. If she fell or sat down suddenly, she would call, "Up, up!" and one of the Bassets would go to her and wait patiently as she pulled herself up. They were all very gentle and affectionate – even with fingers in their eyes or little hands clinging to their ears! Nevertheless, she was never left alone with any dog.

A SUITABLE HOME?

A Basset Hound does not need to live in a mansion, but an apartment that can only be reached by flights of stairs is not

suitable for an adult Basset, let alone a puppy. An eight-week-old puppy can be carried, provided he does not wriggle too much, but a 12-week-old puppy is very heavy. Even if the apartment has a lift, it is equally unsuitable; the other users of the lift are liable to complain, and how will you cope if the power to the lift was cut off for any reason?

You also need to consider the exercise and toilet area; a private garden is no problem, but if a dog is taken to a communal area – where children play – there will be some very serious objections from other members of the community.

Provided that your Basset gets plenty of exercise, he will not care

If you join a breed club, you will get the opportunity to meet lots of like-minded Basset people.

if it is along a town street or a country road. It is best not to walk a young Basset for a long distance along a pavement or road until the growth plates have fused. For further information about exercise, *see Chapter Five: The Best of Care*.

If you have a garden of your own, you will need to consider how much your garden means to you. Part of the historical function of a Basset was to dig into dens and burrows to catch prey, so a Basset Hound will dig. Another historical function was to push through undergrowth to drive the game towards the hunter, so a Basset Hound does not find a hedge much of a barrier. Not only has the garden to be escape-proof, it also has to be made safe for your Basset Hound. *See Chapter Four: The New Arrival*.

THE PERFECT COMPANION
Once a Basset Hound is fully grown, he can be a tireless walker, whether it be on the beach where he can chase the seagulls and sneeze at the stones, the forest

where he can explore the undergrowth and find the rabbit burrows, or the route to the shops, sniffing every lamppost and corner on the way.

If you go for a regular early-morning run, your Basset Hound will enjoy running with you. If you like to go hiking along the highways and byways, your Basset will enjoy it, too; if you enjoy camping or caravanning, so will your Basset. Provided a Basset has suffered no growth injuries and is not allowed to get fat, he has enormous stamina and any type of exercise you favour will be exactly what your Basset Hound will want to do too.

However, if your favourite method of relaxation is sitting on a riverbank and fishing, your Basset will be quite happy to sit with you – for a while – then he will eventually find it boring and wander off to investigate some interesting smells. A long length of rope tied to your Basset's collar or harness, with the other end tied to a fence post, or similar, might be worth considering here.

Or you can purchase a tie-out stake that screws into the ground (see page 56).

When on a scent, the Basset Hound becomes deaf and daft – the scent is all. In this situation, he may suddenly realise he is lost, and he is just as likely to panic as to sensibly track himself back to the place from which he started. Consequently, if you are in a new environment, you must be vigilant or your Basset could easily end up lost.

A Basset can also be something of a couch potato – if you let him be. However, it is best – for the both of you – to get out on a regular basis. A Basset enjoys using his nose and 'reading' the signs on his walk, and his walk is good for you, too – even if it is raining.

The Basset is not built to be a lap dog – but he likes to think he could be. Despite his short legs he can easily climb on to the sofa or your favourite chair. This should be discouraged, not only because he will shed hair, which will then be collected on to your own clothes, but because it can cause some damage to the growth of the limbs in a very young hound. The problem is not so much getting up on the furniture - it is the getting down (see page 69).

A Basset Hound can negotiate stairs, though they do come down faster than they go up! In the early days, steps and stairs can cause damage to the front legs. A safety stair-gate (as used for a child) is a very wise precaution. A reputable breeder will refuse to sell a puppy to someone who lives in an apartment where the only access is by stairs.

JOINING A BREED CLUB

If you want to find out more about Basset Hounds – or you want to get more out of your own Basset – the best plan is to join a breed club. There are many benefits - from fun days and organised walks to promoting welfare and health issues, as well as working towards safeguarding the future of the breed. Membership falls into two categories:

• **Pet owners**, who enjoy the companionship their pet Basset gives them. Both owner and hound can enjoy meeting others and maybe give and receive a little help and/or support when needed.

BASSETS AS THERAPY DOGS

The work of therapy dogs – who visit schools, hospitals, residential homes, and even prisons with their owners – is now widely recognised.

The most important and distinctive characteristic of a therapy dog must be his temperament. A good therapy dog must be friendly, patient, confident, gentle, and comfortable with all situations. They must enjoy human contact and be happy to be petted and handled, sometimes albeit a little awkwardly, which may not suit a young, impressionable Basset.

The temperament of an older Basset, with his laid-back calm and affectionate disposition makes an ideal therapy dog, and there are a number of Bassets and their owners who provide a very valuable service to the community.

- **The show fraternity** where everyone who takes that road sees something special in the breed, or is drawn to the uniqueness of the Basset Hound. They also have an underlying wish to preserve that special something that sets the Basset Hound apart from all other breeds.

A breed club may be involved in the following activities:
- Helping to set the Standard for the breed. This is the written blueprint that describes the 'perfect' Basset Hound. It is the bible of breeders, judges and exhibitors who are striving to produce and promote the best specimens of the breed.

- Drawing up a code of ethics to promote responsible breeding.
- Organising breed shows.
- Organising fun days and Basset walks.
- Putting on educational seminars for anyone wishing to expand their knowledge of the breed.
- Staging scenting or tracking days where you can test your

WORKING WITH BASSETS

Everyone takes a dog into the family expecting the dog to become the family pet. With a Basset Hound it does not work quite like that. A Basset Hound can be more than just a pet dog in the house - a Basset can be a friend and a companion; one can do and share things with a Basset Hound. For his pleasure, and your own, you are likely to find yourself drawn to special events, such as a breed club scenting day, where you can test your Basset's natural ability without the need for lengthy training.

This project was originally masterminded by Cathy Whitehead, who wanted to prove to the sceptics that the Basset Hound was still able to carry out the task that it was bred for, particularly as the Kennel Club in the UK continually stresses that a dog must be 'fit for life and fit for purpose'.

Cathy attended a Bloodhound trial training day to see how this activity could be adapted for Bassets. After months of discussions with the breed club committee, a variation on the theme was agreed and the first scenting day was launched.

"The day dawned and it was absolutely the worst day possible," says Cathy. "It was pouring with rain, blowing a gale and very cold (this was July!), but we had arranged it and as we had not asked for prepaid entries, we could not cancel.

"About 12 dogs turned up, and the rain stopped for long enough to allow everyone to have a go. We had time to spend with the slow learners to enable everyone to at least make an attempt. We were so proud to have achieved something that had not been done before."

"The following year, for the first time, we tried a quarter-mile line over rough plough and on a shaped route. We *almost* had one Basset Hound complete this course – though he got distracted about 50 yards from the end – but this was such an achievement for our breed, which has been much maligned over the last few years as being not able to work over rough plough or being able to follow a scent.

"If our two trials could prove anything, it was: "Yes, they can still do it". The ultimate goal would be to have a Basset Hound Working Champion. Then we can truly say that we (as a club) have made a difference to the dog world."

Basset's ability to follow a track.
- Open discussion with the Kennel Club concerning breed issues.
- It is also the responsibility of breed clubs to help train future judges.

Essentially, a breed club is there to offer support and help to anyone and everyone who needs it – and it is dedicated to those ends.

HELPING OTHERS

It is essential that breed knowledge is handed down from the most experienced to anyone who needs help. Though, in some cases, the most experienced are not always those who have had long years of involvement with the breed clubs.

Whenever you get a group of Basset owners together, the discussion will soon turn to a problem someone has. Most owners are only too pleased to help anyone who finds themselves in difficulties and will always lend a sympathetic ear.

After months of hard work, the first scenting day for Bassets was launched.
Photo © Mike Doolan.

Some Bassets got the idea immediately...
Photo © Mike Doolan.

THE FIRST BASSET HOUNDS

Chapter 2

I t is generally understood that the basic hominid and canid types of mammal appeared around the first Ice Age, roughly two million years ago. These creatures, through a process of genetic change and adaptation, developed further and there is firm evidence of canine/wolf types and early Stone Age man co-existing from about 300,0000 years ago.

Early hominids were hunter-gatherers. Although hunter-gatherers live a hand-to-mouth existence, they still leave some waste in their trail. Canids would have been attracted to the hominids and their camps, by the amount of waste and debris left around.

We may be dog lovers, but we are under no illusions and we know our animals will take the easy option and scavenge if they can.

GATHERING EVIDENCE

From archaeological evidence, about 75,000 years ago – around the time of the last Ice Age – Neanderthal and Cro-Magnon types of man had high-level cultural and social organisations. A family/tribe were able to join together to hunt in a highly structured manner in order to find and kill large and powerful prey. Canid packs also form organised killing groups, using the same stratagems of stalking, herding and cutting out, incorporating a differentiation of labour and the eventual dispersal of the prize amongst the rest of the pack. We have all seen present-day films showing wolf packs still hunting in the same manner.

Canines would have followed the hunts and, inevitably, those that gave the right type of assistance would have been encouraged to join future hunts. Canines would have been tolerated in and around the camps for their services in waste disposal, their reduction of the rodent population, and for their guarding and warning abilities. There is definite evidence of some interaction between canine types and hominid types in the very early Stone Age (around the time of the first Ice Age), and by the time of the last Ice Age (around 75, 000 years ago) there is firm evidence that the Neanderthal and Cro-Magnon types of man were using canid types as guards, companions, and assistants or 'tools' aiding the search for meat. Archaeologists have found canine skulls buried at the entrance to caves used for habitation, and suggest that this was seen as a powerful totem for keeping the dwelling safe when the extended family and their

EARLY HUNTERS

Primitive man hunted in order to live. Cave paintings, executed some 16,000 years ago, at Lascaux, at the very northernmost edge of the Pyrenees in the Dordogne region of France, show early man and early dogs hunting deer – as a partnership. To see the paintings is an experience not to be missed. It is amazing to discover that earliest men could paint such anatomically correct animals – particularly when you bear in mind that the only artificial light would have been produced by burning fats or maybe rushes, and the only materials would have been very primitive earth-pigments to use for paints.

Even more spectacular is the way in which the contours of the rock were used to enhance the paintings – a curve to aid a belly shape, or a lump of rock to bring a head to the fore. It is a most wonderful experience to stand in the total darkness, with a guide illuminating the drawings with a lantern, and look back in time to those very first hunting scenes.

First of all came the 'aptitude' of the canine and then came 'use' by hominids. The relationship evolved with the aptitude becoming a 'requirement' and the requirement becoming a 'necessity'. Human lives could depend upon canine ability.

As weapons – spears and bows and arrows – became more sophisticated and man could select and kill prey from a distance, it became essential that the canines should work together with each other and with the hominids in the selection of the prey. They also needed to recognise simple instructions from the hominids in order to hunt to the best advantage and avoid injury from the weapons. Canines with this ability would be retained and would carry on breeding, fixing the traits down the generations.

Animals, birds, and even fish are known to develop certain differences in appearance within distinct environmental areas, and where there is a definite topographical boundary, such as river or a range of high hills. Canine loyalty to a particular human tribe would have worked in the same way, and eventually there would have been perceptible differences in the appearance of a canine living with his tribe in one area to that of one living with a tribe some miles away.

Man has always favoured that which pleases the senses and – along with the necessity for aptitude – would have come the requirement for 'pleasing the

canines went down to the summer camps.

Excavations have also uncovered burials around what appear to have been 'family hearths'; these mostly contained human remains, but others have contained canine and human or just canine remains. In many of these graves, evidence of flowers is present.

A BREEDING STRATEGY

Initially, the canines would have bred willy-nilly; there would have been no human strategy. Inevitably, those canines that could do a useful job would be

retained and would carry on breeding, while those with no beneficial aptitudes would, no doubt, have been killed and eaten. By such selection – allowing canines with valuable abilities to live – the beneficial traits would become fixed. Men would, no doubt, have also selected breeding stock for their appearance. But looks counted only for so much; ability was of far more importance in the use of what amounted to a 'tool' or 'weapon'. It could make the difference between living and dying – death from attack or death from starvation.

eye'. Canines would be retained for both ability and aesthetic reasons, and a regional type would become fixed. In such ways would the various breeds have evolved.

Selective breeding and regional differences eventually produced great variances in the appearance of those canids adopted by mankind and, by around 6,000 years ago, there were already prominent canine experts in Egypt, and four distinct pure breeds clearly featured in Egyptian art.

We know from writings, paintings and artifacts of ancient peoples that very distinct 'types' of dog had emerged, and these would be used as barter and trade goods. Dogs with the greater ability to do a specific job would be of far more value than those with a lesser ability. As civilisations grew and there was greater ease and comfort, particularly amongst the richer societies, the appearance of the dogs would count almost as much as ability. The Romans, Egyptians, Phoenicians and early Chinese were all known to have 'traded' or 'gifted' specific breed types of dogs.

THE FIRST SCENTHOUNDS

Xenophon (430-355BC), a Greek soldier and scholar, became an enthusiastic dog breeder and huntsman following his retirement from military

Dogs have been used to assist with the hunt from the earliest of times. A Syrian Bas relief, c. 668-628BC.

duties. His perfect hunting dog, the Castor-dog, was used in packs for hunting hare. They hunted by scent and would go off in full cry, followed by the huntsman on foot. These dogs, from his descriptions, were small types, very similar to present-day Beagles. This is the first documented evidence of hunting as a sport. Evidence of a Basset type of dog comes much later.

In the excavations of an ancient harbour area of Pisa, in Tuscany, a skeleton of a man with an outstretched arm was discovered, and laid across the arm is the skeleton of a dog with a large

body and short twisted legs; the date of the material is about 10AD.

In Britain, archaeologists excavating occupation of a Roman garrison of Corbridge Station in Northumberland found a number of dogs that have been identified as Basset types and small Greyhounds. They are dated around 80-120AD.

FORMAL HUNTING WITH HOUNDS

Hunting with dogs was a necessity of mankind for many thousands of years, but it was in France that the royalty, nobility and clergy developed the 'art' of hunting with hounds. Hubert (656-727), a cleric and a son of the Duc de Guienne, hunted in the Ardennes region. It has gone down in folklore that he was the instigator of the 'art' of the hunt, although the techniques were well developed by his time.

It is also popularly supposed that the St Hubert hounds were of a definite and uniform type – similar to the Bloodhound – and that all scenthounds were developed from this unique race. However, it is documented that Hubert selected his hounds for their hunting ability alone. Chronicles from the time demonstrate that the 'Huberts' were of very mixed type and, apart from the superb working qualities, they were not bred 'true' in appearance.

Nevertheless, because these hounds had a great reputation as hunters, they were in demand nationwide and were welcome additions to any pack.

In order to retain this important aptitude for the chase, great thought and care was given to the breeding of individual packs, which would eventually become known by the name of their owners, or of the region they hunted in. The huntsmen bred and selected not only for hunting proficiency, but also for health and strength. Whether hunting for sport or the necessity to put food on the table, only dogs with the right abilities would be used. They were bred to hunt; it did not matter how attractive the animal looked, if he was not capable of hunting successfully, he was not retained in the pack. The same holds true today.

Although the appearance of the animal was secondary to the capability, inevitably, each huntsman's individual tastes and preferences of colour and conformation led to the development of several distinct breeds of hound which were put against the various types of game in different regions. By the time of the French Revolution, in the late 18th century, more than 40 breeds and varieties of hound were known in France.

Several of the breeds came in three sizes: the full-sized Chien d'Ordre standing about 23-30 inches (58-76 cms) at the shoulder; the Briquet, which is a medium-sized hound, being more compact, shorter coupled and standing at about 15-23 inches (38-58 cms) at the shoulder; then, finally, the Basset standing 10-15 inches (25.5-38 cms) at the shoulder.

BASSET TYPES

According to a famous French huntsman, Le Comte Le Couteulx de Canteleu, writing in his manual *De Venerie Francaise* published in the late 1800s, a 16th century huntsman, Du Fouilloux, had a great preference for using the Basset – or shorter-legged type of dog – to hunt fox and badger; they were used more like terriers and put to ground after the prey. Du Fouilloux recognised two types:

"The crook legged type with short coats who, being less excitable, are better for badger as they stay down longer, and the more excitable types with straight legs and rough coats… (probably related to what we know today as the Basset Griffon Vendeen) *…who will hunt above ground like regular hounds or go to ground with great keenness, though*

The Bloodhound traces its roots back to St Hubert Hounds, which were famed for their hunting ability.

FRENCH HOUNDS
In France, a shorter-legged hound was preferred for hunting fox and badger.

Petit Basset Griffon Vendeen.

Basset Fauve de Bretagne.

Basset Hound.

Basset Bleu de Gascogne.

A Beagle was mated to one of the early French imports.

obliged to come up sooner for air; the drawback to this type being that they are over bold - having a tendency to fight the fox or badger instead of driving him out."

Basset types, especially the full crook type, have been popular in France since the 1680s as a superior hound for the "chasse a tir" – a method of hunting game whereby the short-legged hound was able to go through the dense undergrowth and flush out the quarry ready for the waiting sportsmen to shoot, as some gundogs do today. Bassets with the full crook, "Bassets a jambes torses", were considered superior to their Basset cousins with straight legs "Bassets a jambes droites" because they were slower moving and thus did not push the quarry too quickly, frightening it into escape. The prey, usually rabbit, hare or deer, were driven slowly but surely away from the slow-moving but probably noisy hounds to give an easy shot for the waiting guns, which, in the very early days of this type of shooting, were very cumbersome. More menacing game, such as wild boar and wolf, were also hunted by this method in order to try to control their numbers and so prevent their dangerous attacks and devastation of crops and livestock.

Basset breeds have traditionally been used in France to drive the game to within reach of the guns without frightening or hurrying it; it was only prior to the Second World War that the French recognised the 'astonishing' fact that Bassets could catch a hare without the need for guns! Some Bassets in France are still used singly as gundogs, a few are dual-purpose.

A NEW TYPE EMERGES

Le Comte Le Couteulx de Canteleu, in his writings, indicates the Bassets Artésien had become almost extinct by the early 1870s and both he and a Monsieur Lane had, using almost the same stock, reformed the breed. However, the Comte obviously did not care much for the 'Lane type', thinking them to be too high and too crooked in the leg. The Comte, as much as possible, only selected hounds with straight legs as breeding stock, as crooked-legged to crooked-legged tended "to produce hounds which cannot walk at all".

Hounds bred by Monsieur Lane were not only taller than the 'Canteleu type', they were also heavier and lighter in colour, being mostly a very pale tan (lemon) and white. The difference in head was very marked between the two types – the 'Lanes' being tight in skin, with lips cut away fairly sharply, and a distinct lack of flews. The eyes appeared prominent and quite yellow in colour. However, it was in the ear properties where they had their greatest qualities. The leathers were set on low and of great length and suppleness to give the characteristic inward curl of the Basset Artésien.

THE FIRST BASSET HOUNDS

French hounds first arrived in England in 1866 when Lord Galway acquired a male and female from the Marquis de Tournaon. They were not the same as the Basset Hounds we see today, being lighter in body and swifter of foot. Lord Galway mated them in 1867 then sold the two hounds and their five offspring to Lord Onslow in the early 1870s. Lord Onslow's pack was strengthened by further imports of Bassets Artésien from the kennels of Le Comte Le

HOUNDSTONE MADELAINE MAY: A SHOW BASSET AND A GUNDOG

Madelaine May has had a successful showing career, gaining two Challenge Certificates, a Best in Show at Westbury Canine Society, and numerous other awards, but she prefers to fit her showing career around her gundog duties. Here is her story, told by Rob Coulbert, who is a marksmen employed to control the deer population.

"My first inkling of the improbable being not only probable but here in the room with me was brought about when my rifle fell out of the gun cabinet and clanged the telescopic sight into the floor. I had just been called by a local farmer, who urgently required me to explain to some deer that grazing off the newly sprouting maize plants was a very bad idea. So a quick trip out to the hills to reset my scope was my main priority. My wife, however, reminded me that I had promised to take the Bassets out for a walk. Without giving it much thought, I piled the hounds into the car, as well as my rifle and a couple of targets.

"I asked my wife, Pam, to walk off a few metres behind me, and I set my rifle up toward the targets 100 metres away. A big loud bang ensued, followed by the sound of a Basset stampede behind me. There were four Basset noses sticking out from under the Range Rover, but one puppy, staring intently at the target, sat rock steady just behind me. Madelaine Basset was keen to see what was going on.

"I took her out with me to walk the hedges after a rabbit or maybe even a pheasant. Not only did she get the hang of staying to heel when told, but pretty rapidly realised that some crafty wildlife actually stayed put as we walked past. The work needed to chase these critters out from the shrubbery came quickly and easily to Mad Basset, and I soon saw that the silly-looking ears function well as armour on the foreleg and front flank when pushing hard to penetrate gorse and brambles. She also showed me that the best way into big holly clumps on the stream banks is to swim under them and push the pheasants out from the middle. Retrieving is not on. That is what I am there for, according to Mad Basset. Any weather, any type of terrain, and she can easily outwork my gamekeeper friend's supposedly superior gundog.

"Due to my own stupidity, I allowed Madelaine to jump out of the back of the Range Rover on to a steeply sloping grass bank. The resulting back injury was very nearly fatal, but thanks to Langford Veterinary College's expertise and kindness, Mad Basset can still show the rest of the canine family how to work a hedge. Maybe not as fast or for as long as before, but if a gun is seen in close proximity to the door, I am given clear Basset-style instructions on the logical choice of shooting companion, and she has been a good and reliable helpmate. Good girl!"

Couteulx de Canteleu.

Sir Everett Millais acquired some of the Onslow hounds, and also imported a hound named 'Model' from the same French kennel. Model was mated to a Beagle bitch. A daughter, Dina, was mated back to her sire, and two of the resulting puppies looked like purebred Bassets – Millais had some success with them in the show ring. Lord

Onslow mated one of his own bitches to Model and paid the stud fee with a puppy bitch called Garenne. Mr G.R. Krehl acquired a Millais bitch called Kathleen, and in 1880 he imported a male hound from Le Comte Le Couteulx de Canteleu named Fino de Paris. This dog was widely used at stud and had a great impact on the Basset breed in England. Fino de Paris

had a head more like the Bloodhound rather than the 'Foxhoundish' head of Millais's Model.

In 1883/4, Mr Krehl, along with other enthusiasts, formed the Basset Club. Mr Krehl listed the points and a description of the breed and this was accepted at a meeting in 1899.

By the 1890s the Basset Artesians in this country had become very

BREED DESCRIPTION 1899

The Basset Hound Club logo.

POINTS OF THE BASSET HOUND (SMOOTH) 1899	VALUE
Head, Skull, Eyes, Muzzle, and Flews	15
Ears	15
Neck, Dewlap, Chest, and Shoulders	10
Fore Legs and Feet	15
Back, Loins, and Hindquarters	10
Stern	5
Coat and Skin	10
Colour and Markings	15
'Basset Character' and Symmetry	5
Total	**100**

GENERAL APPEARANCE

1. To begin with the Head as the most distinguishing part of all breeds. The head of the Basset-hound is most perfect when it closest resembles a Bloodhound's. It is long and narrow, with heavy flews, occiput prominent, "la bosse de la chasse", and forehead wrinkled to the eyes, which should be kind and show the

inbred, producing Bassets lacking size and bone. A Mr Marsden from Leeds crossed his Basset Artesians with Bloodhounds; two years later, Sir Everett Millais, having previously had success with Beagle crosses, also crossed his hounds with the Bloodhound via artificial insemination. A further Bloodhound influence was brought into the breed by Mrs Elms of the Reynalton kennel in the mid 1900s. By this time there was a distinct difference between the various purebred Basset breeds of the French and the Bassets bred in England.

Because of the difficulties caused by the First World War, the enthusiasm for a Basset breed club subsided and it was disbanded in 1921. Some enthusiasts continued to show, but it was those who continued to hunt with their hounds that we should thank for retaining the true breed characteristics. Major Heseltine and his wife imported a couple of French hounds to join their Walhampton pack, as they – and a number of other avid sportsmen – were very unhappy with the show-type of Basset. As a result, they formed their own club – the Masters of Basset Hounds Association.

haw. The general appearance of the head must present high breeding and reposeful dignity; the teeth are small, and the upper jaw sometimes protrudes. This is not a fault, and is called the "bec de lievre".

2. The Ears very long, and when drawn forward folding well over the nose - so long that in hunting they will often actually tread on them; they are set on low, and hang loose in folds like drapery, the ends inward curling, in texture thin and velvety.

3. The Neck is powerful, with heavy dewlaps. Elbows must not turn out. The chest is deep, full, and framed like a "man-of-war". Body long and low.

4. Fore Legs short, about 4-in., and close-fitting to the chest till the crooked knee, from where the wrinkled ankle ends in a massive paw, each toe standing out distinctly.

5. The Stifles are bent, and the quarters full of muscle, which stands out so that when one looks at the dog from behind, it gives him a round, barrel-like effect. This, with their peculiar, waddling gait, goes a long way towards Basset character, a quality easily recognised by the judge, and as desirable as Terrier character in a Terrier.

6. The Stern is coarse underneath, and carried hound-fashion.

7. The Coat is short, smooth, and fine, and has a gloss on it like that of a racehorse. (To get this appearance, they should be hound-gloved, never brushed.) Skin loose and elastic.

8. The Colour should be black, white, and tan; the head, shoulders, and quarters a rich tan, and black patches on the back. They are also sometimes hare-pied.

Catalogue of the Basset Hound Show 1918.

27

LOST BREEDS

LOST BREEDS

Bassets from the Artois (Basset Artésiens) and Normandy (Basset Normands) regions have, to all intents and purposes, been lost as specific breeds. In the early part of the 20th century, a Monsieur Verrier combined the two breeds and, along with other like-minded French breeders, formed a society for the Basset Artésien-Normand breed.

The head properties of the hounds incline more to the 'Norman' type rather than the 'Artois' type, but they have the 'Artois' ears with the soft, inward curl, which is preferred, rather than the flat 'Norman' ear leather sometimes still seen in our Bassets.

HUNTING WITH BASSET HOUNDS

It is generally accepted that the Basset Hound as we know it originated in France, where its low stature enabled it to work in thick cover, to flush game to guns. In the UK, however, since the late 19th century, the Basset Hound has traditionally been used in a pack, to hunt its quarry by scent. Prior to the passing of the Hunting Act 2004, that quarry was usually hare, although Bassets have been used to hunt other quarry, such as roe deer. Hunting with Basset Hounds in the UK is governed by the Masters of Basset Hounds Association (MBHA), which has a number of registered (member) packs, including ones in the United States and in Spain.

Huntsman Peter Guy describes the current hunting scene in the UK:

"The majority of Basset packs operating within the UK use one of two types of hound. The first is simply referred to as a Basset Hound. It is a short-legged hound, long in body and long in ear, smooth of coat. It is not a small hound; it is a large hound on short legs. The second type is known as the English Basset. This is essentially a hunting hound, and you are unlikely to see one being walked in your local park. By comparison with the Basset Hound, it is likely to be rather longer in the leg and shorter in the ear. Somewhere in its ancestry will be a longer-legged hound, such as a harrier.

"We first began hunting because we loved the Basset Hound as a breed, and felt it essential that we should experience it doing what comes naturally. Let me emphasise that – contrary to what you may be told – hounds do not have to be taught to hunt. In most cases it is as necessary as eating, drinking and sleeping, which, let's face it, are all very important in a Basset's life! If you love Basset Hounds, you, too, should take the opportunity to see them hunt.

"The other attractions of hunting with Bassets are, first of all, that it is carried out on foot, so you require no specialised equipment or clothing beyond that which you would require for a walk in the countryside. Secondly, Basset Hounds tend to be slower than other breeds of hound, so are that bit easier to follow. Note that I said 'slower' and not 'slow', as many people following Bassets for the first time are surprised by their turn of speed. For me, one of the outstanding qualities of the Basset Hound is his glorious voice – and you don't need to be a hunting expert to appreciate that. You do possibly need a little experience to appreciate another of his qualities: his superb scenting ability, which enables him to hunt when other breeds would struggle."

AFTER THE SECOND WORLD WAR

Just after the Second World War the Basset Hound in England had, once more, become very inbred and undesirable characteristics were emerging. Miss Peggy Keevil, who hunted with her own pack – the famous Grims Basset Hounds – imported three Bassets Artesien-Normand from France. She was very lucky to acquire them, considering the state of the country after the German occupation and subsequent fighting during the invasion and liberation of France.

Ulema de Barly had particular impact on the breed. Not only was he a great hunting hound and a wonderful showman (winning Best of Breed at Crufts in 1951), but he

The Basset is still used as a hunting hound, working in a pack.
Photo © Peter Guy.

The working Basset is longer in the leg than those bred as show and companion dogs.

Grims Ulema de Barly: A superb hunter and a great showman.

Ch. Blaby Hal: A show Champion who also gained his hunt certificate.

Ch. Maycombe Merryman.

Basset Hound Club Show 1986: Jim Grey (left) with Ch. Norendo Amazing Grace winning Best of Breed and Ann Roberts (right) with Ch. Lodway Lancer of Islwyn, Reserve Best of Breed. The judges are Margaret Thorley and Joan Izard. *Roger Chambers Photography.*

also sired good-looking hounds carrying the same abilities. Most Basset Hounds today can trace their ancestry back to him.

Due to the improvements in the health and conformation of the breed, there was renewed enthusiasm from both working and showing devotees. In May 1954, the Basset Hound Club was formed by a number of Basset owners, including Miss Keevil. Kennel Club recognition soon followed. A number of the Basset Hound Club members owned their own private packs of Basset Hounds and hunted

them regularly, inviting other members of the Basset Hound Club to follow the pack.

In 1957, three years after the reformation of the Basset Hound Club, it was agreed that the breed in Great Britain was once again becoming far too inbred, and it would be beneficial for the breed to bring a pure-bred stallion hound into the country to use on members' bitches. It was decided that an American hound would be a suitable outcross and members Miss Keevil and Mrs Jagger were given the task of finding such a suitable

stallion hound. Unfortunately, no one would sell a top-winning adult stud dog.

American doyenne of the breed, Peg Walton, had whelped a litter on 14 August 1958, in which there was a puppy dog she was prepared to sell to the Basset Hound Club. This was Lyn Mar Acres Dauntless, a mottled tricolour, who cost 250 dollars. He was kept at the Grims' kennels at the Basset Hound Club's expense and he was for the use, at stud, of club members. Unfortunately, he was considered too 'American' for the majority of breeders and judges in England, and so was sold to Miss Keevil. George Johnston of the famous Sykemoor kennel then imported a tricolour Artesian-Normand dog puppy, Hercule de L'Ombree, in 1959.

The Grims' hounds were regularly hunted and club members were welcomed to follow the pack. As a result of Miss Keevil's retirement from the club in 1969, the Basset Hound Club members who wished to continue to hunt formed their own purebred Basset pack – the Albany – and members, with the permission of the Master, were able to enter their own hound into the pack and hunt them. A famous Basset to gain his hunt certificate was Doreen Gilberthope's Show Champion Blaby Hal, who was a magnificent animal.

THE MODERN ERA
Many of the Basset Hounds currently seen in the British show ring look, to the specialist eye, quite different to those of the 1970s and 1980s, which now appear old fashioned. Whether or not this has been caused by the hunting ban in 2004 is debatable but, certainly, in the late 1980s and 1990s, Bassets were beginning to be pictured by the general, non-showing owner more as uniquely amusing, cuddly pets than as hunters. The growing emergence of puppy farmers and cash crop breeders in Wales and elsewhere provided many more Bassets for the British urban household than those that had been carefully bred by the breed enthusiasts. The unique conformation of dwarf legs and normal-sized body and head began

Colin and Trish Wells with some Kortebin Bassets.
Photo © Jon Day.

Representatives of the Fivevalleys Bassets.

to be eroded. Legs became ever shorter; wrinkles and loose skin became rather excessive, and the body length shortened – perhaps trying to make the Basset look to be more in proportion, rather like a 'normal' dog.

There are few breeder/exhibitors remaining from the 1970s. Moonsmead Bassets are still shown and bred by Rosemary Izard Corbett, who carried on the line from her mother, Joan; Dennis and Margaret Ledward still exhibit the Drawdell Basset Hounds; Jim and Marianne Nixon breed and exhibit the Brackenacre Hounds; Mrs Veronica Ross still has her Verwood Bassets, though she no longer shows them, and Colin and Trish Wells breed and exhibit their Kortebin Bassets.

From the 1980s we still have the Tanneron Bassets, shown and bred by Nigel Luxmore-Ball who took over the affix from his mother, Felicity. The Nedlaw Bassets are still occasionally bred and exhibited by Patience and Patrick Walden, though they are now more involved with Beagles. Elizabeth Watson still occasionally exhibits her Carresmar Bassets. The Balmacara Bassets of Francis and Ron Meredith are also occasionally seen in the show ring. Sandra Thexton is still breeding and having success with her Barrenger Bassets. Later in the 1980s came Mrs Jo Freer's Switherland Bassets, the affix later co-owned with husband Phil. Both Jo and Phil retain their interest in the affix, but it is now Phil who exhibits the Switherland Bassets with his partner, Marita Rodgers.

From the 1990s we have Sandra Allen exhibiting her Fivevalley's Bassets, and Malcolm Ellrich with his Malrich Bassets. Mr and Mrs Johnston are still breeding and exhibiting the Burnvale Bassets. After a spell living abroad, Bill O'Loughlin returned to England with his Bassbarrs – only to leave England again in the early 2000s. He and the Bassbarrs returned to England in 2010. Mr and Mrs Storton are exhibiting the Dereheath Bassets, and Mr and Mrs Tryhorn are still seen in the ring with the Moragden Bassets.

From the mid-1990s we have Dave and Clare Darley (Clavidar), Mrs Debbie Newman (Woferlow) and Tina Watkins (Blackvein) all continuing to breed and show their Basset Hounds. From the turn of the century, the Kelsey family have had success with the Malacante Bassets, and Phil McGarry-Arthurs from Northern Ireland has had success with his Faburn Bassets.

There are many more people exhibiting their home-bred Basset Hounds – many of which are doing very well in the show ring.

THE BASSET HOUND IN AMERICA

We are fortunate in having Col. Robert E. Booth (ret.) to provide some highlights on Basset Hound activity in America from the 1950s through to the present day. A Basset Hound judge, he authored The Official Book of the Basset Hound at the request of the Basset Hound Club of America. What follows will hopefully give you a feel for the American Basset Hound today and how the breed arrived there.

During the 1950s, most breedings in America appeared to have been planned with sole emphasis on phenotypical considerations: that is, based primarily on the 'look' and/or 'style' of some of the stronger kennels worldwide. These kennels included: Grims, Sykemoor, Rossingham, Notrenom, Belbay, Lyn Mar Acres and Santana-Mandeville. Of course, there were others as well, such as Belleau, Millvan, Hess, Le Chenil, Look's, Lime Tree, En-Hu, Hubertus, Norman's, Siefenjagenheim, Blue Hill, Hartshead, Nancy Evans', Sherlitt's, Braun, Long View Acres, The Ring's, Barnspark, and Double B's.

Most breeders today would be hard put to go any further back in Basset history than the Lyn Mar Acres and Santana-Mandeville days – two of the most influential kennels. Lyn Mar Acres was the kennel prefix of Margaret and M. Lynwood Walton (Peg & Woody), located in New Jersey, while for the most part, Paul and Helen Nelson of Santana-Mandeville were in California. Sadly, many of the foregoing breeders are not alive today.

THE SIXTIES

In the 1960s, many more breeders established kennels. Some were a flash in the pan, while others made it through the long haul.

Of these 1960s entrants, Kazoo Kennels, Reg (Mary Jo Shields) would become well known for producing hounds that carried a great deal of type. Manor Hill (Joan Scholz) certainly added structural

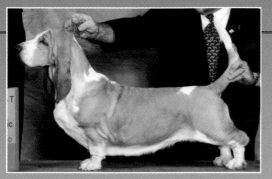

Am. Ch. Topsfield Vision Silver Noodles. Breeders: Nancy Richmond, Lisa Brackett, Anne Testoni and Bjorn Zetterlund. Owners: Claudia Orlandi, Claire Steidel, Nancy Richmond, Anne Testoni and Bjorn Zetterlund. Top-winning bitch, (22 Bests in Show) in breed history. *Photographer: Melia.*

Am. Ch. Splash's The Professor. Breeders: Bill, Jo Ann & Jackie Nolan. Owners/Co-owners: Breeders and Shirley & Arthur Ponsart. Multiple Best in Show Winner. *Photographer: Tom Nutting.*

Am. Ch. Castlehill's Ace in the Hole at Sasquatch. Breeders: Whitney Wetmore, Jim & Sharon Dok & Sarah Broom. Owners: Bobbi Brandt & Donna Coker. Best in Junior Sweepstakes winner at the Basset Hound Club of America National Specialty 2009 *Photographer: Elaine.*

Am. Ch. Birnam's Killian of Kaizen. Breeders: Norman and Mary Ann Wiginton, Lora Megli and Julie Strauss. Owners: Norman and Mary Ann Wiginton. Award of Merit at the Basset Hound Club of America National Specialty 2008 *Photographer: Nugent.*

Am. Grand Ch. BoBac Boss's Grand Canyon. Breeders/Owners: Richard and Sharon Nance. Co-owners: Miles and Martha Fairris. A very young dog, always owner handled, but already a Grand Champion with multiple BOB wins. *Photographer: Thomas.*

Am. Ch. Baywind-Craigwood Smokin in Havana. Breeders: Michael and Debbie Moore. Owners: Breeders and Sandra Campbell. A young dog, already a multiple Specialty winner, Group placer and an Award of Merit at the 2010 BHCA National Specialty.

Photographer: Susan & Lennah.

Am. Ch. Topsfield Bumper Cars, ROM, CD.
Breeder/Owner: Claudia Orlandi, PhD – Topsfield.
Basset Hound Club of America National
Specialty Best of Breed 2003. Numerous Breed,
Group and Best in Show awards.
Photographer: Ashbey.

Ch. By-U-Cal's Razzle Dazzle. Breeders/Owners:
Steve and Sharon Calhoun. Co-owners: Alyce &
Richard Gilmore. BHCA National Specialty Best of
Breed winner 1996 and 1998. BHCA National
Specialty Best of Opposite Sex winner 1997. She
had an amazing show career. *Photographer: Cook.*

soundness to the mix. Northwood's (Don Martin & family) were as responsible as anyone for introducing 'showmanship' to Basset Hound breed competition. One of the sons, Bryan, is a top professional handler today. The Musicland kennel of (then) Jean Dudley produced well over 100 Champions. Oranpark (Wilton and Mary Meyer) did a great job of carrying on the Santana-Mandeville line.

Magem Hills (Marg and John Patterson) bred some fine hounds. The Abbot Run Valley dogs of Marge and Walter Brandt were some of the best in this time period. The Coralwood kennels (Bill Barton) produced a number of very good dogs. Bill celebrated his 50th year of BHCA membership by judging Best of Breed at the 2010 BHCA National Specialty.

THE SEVENTIES
The 1970s witnessed the emergence of a large number of new kennels.

During this period a number of these kennels distinguished themselves with their hounds. The Tal-E-Ho kennels of Ann and Henry Jerman was one such kennel. Beaujangles Bassets, co-owned by Diane Malenfant and Claudia Lane, was another. Sandra Campbell's Craigwood kennels became well known for the quality of her bitches, and this still remains true today. The Stoneybluff Bassets of Virginia and Frank Kovalic established a very specific style of hound by following line breeding based on the Lyn Mar Acres kennel.

THE EIGHTIES
The 1980s saw many additional kennel names surface, and several of them are still in the mix today.

The Hiflite kennel (Bob and Mary Jane Booth) began an active breeding programme again when Bob finally retired from the military. They bred Ch. Hiflite Briarcrest Extra Man, later owned by Knox and Bette Williams. Call named 'Butch', this stud dog went on to become the top producer in the history of the breed with 67 titled offspring. Other kennels that may have started earlier actually came into their own during this time. Some of those were Briarcrest, Castlehill, Ambrican, Fort Merrill, Sanchu, Branscombe, First Class, Bone-A-Part, Stonewall, Chasan and Woodhaven.

THE NINETIES
The dawn of the 1990s saw a distinct downtrend in the number of participants entering into the sport at this juncture. This is not limited to just Basset Hounds, but seems to extend across the entire spectrum.

**Am. Ch. Courtyard's Kreggo of Hiflite.
Breeders: Hiflite Kennels, Reg. & Doris M.
Courtney. Owners: Hiflite Kennels, Reg.
(Robert E. & Mary Jane Booth). A multiple
BHCA Specialty Best of Breed winner.**

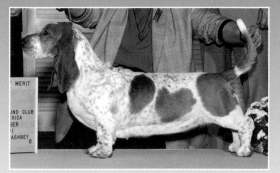

**Am. Ch. Craigwood Tickery Dickery Dot.
Breeder: Sandra Campbell. Owners: Sandra
Campbell & Heidi Martin. Basset Hound Club of
America National Specialty Award of Merit
winner 1991.** *Photographer: Ashbey.*

We are finding fewer and fewer young people developing an interest in breeding or showing. It seems that the majority of the newcomers just want to purchase a hound and have an instant winner! Of course, some of this problem can be attributed to the downturn in the worldwide economy. Unfortunately, few new names have surfaced during the first decade of the 2000s.

THE CURRENT SCENE

Some of the somewhat newer kennels continued to progress during the past two decades (1990-2010). The good news is that we have experienced a renewed interest in other disciplines, such as field trials, obedience, agility, rally, tracking and the newer hunt test. GFCh. Pettit's Ranger Ric still holds the record as the all-time top-producing Field Trial Champion sire with a phenomenal 47 Field

Champions to his credit. Showing that conformation hounds can work in the field as well are dogs from kennels such as Slippery Hill, Branscombe and Tailgate.

Obedience Bassets came into their own in the early 1960s, heralded by Buzz Taylor and his Bridlespur Nudger, UD, who was number one obedience Basset for seven years! Some kennels that have done well in obedience and tracking over the years are Bugle Bay, Branscombe and Misty Meadows. The BeeLee Bassets of Billy and Lena Wray set an impressive tracking record by finishing 19 hounds. Agility, rally and the hunt test are, relatively, too new yet to have generated any consistent big winners, but the Kaleidoscope Bassets of Ellen Ferguson seem to be leading the pack.

In my mind, the most important thing to have happened within the

Basset Hound Club of America during this past decade has been the renewed interest and emphasis in the area of breeder and judges' education. The education committee chair, Dr. Claudia Orlandi (Topsfield), and her committee have developed programmes and methods that have been widely accepted by the membership and the American Kennel Club as well. She and her committee members have, over the decade, developed the concept of The Basset Hound University. This consists of a series of booklets that are Basset Hound-specific and cover the 'how to' in all aspects of the sport, starting with the ABCs of breeding.

I can certainly see an overall improvement in a larger number of dogs being shown today. Certainly, a significant portion of this improvement can be directly

Aus. Grand Ch. Beauchasseur Allo Allo. Owned by Chris Lawrence. *Photographer: Haseldine.*

NZ & Aus. Ch. Bayparque Potawatomi ('Leggo'). Bred and owned by Jill Brooker, former Secretary Vice President of the Basset Hound Club of New Zealand.

attributed to the educational programmes. Very deservedly, in 2009, Claudia Orlandi was selected by the American Kennel Club as AKC's Breeder of the Year.

The photos I have selected depict a number of American Basset Hounds who have completed their AKC Championships from 2000 onwards. These are excellent examples of the breed with great toplines, good angulation, balanced structure and excellent breed type. We hope you will enjoy, evaluate and compare them in appreciation of this wonderful breed.

AUSTRALIA

Early Bassets introduced to Australia died out before the start of the 20th Century; they were reintroduced in the late 1950s. Veterinarian, Harry Spira, his wife Margaret, Eileen McInolty and Ruth Matthews of the Dubrovnick kennel, Eileen's son John (and his wife Judy) enlisted the help of a visiting judge called McDonald Daly. He agreed to scout

around for suitable hounds to import. With his help they obtained, from Peggy Keevil, a British dog – Grims Vanquish – and a "relatively non-related bitch", Grims Caroline, who was in whelp (the princely sum paid for Caroline was £25 or £30). Caroline whelped a litter of 10 or 11 in quarantine. She was somewhat "uncertain" in temperament and so, too, were a number of her progeny. Vanquish had a wonderful temperament.

Another bitch, Bockleton Country Maid, was imported – "very gentle and sweet in her temperament, she introduced a much greater degree of soundness than we had ever had before…" Then came British-bred Fochno hounds Cherry, Conker and Chestnut, from Mrs J Lorton, and, although from the same kennel, they were not too closely related. Then came Dauphin, more of a French 'type', who was entirely different to any other import to Australia, being "…plainer, sounder and tighter… he came out at the

right time." Dauphin was greatly used on Australian bitches, because he was the only dog with totally unrelated bloodlines.

Harry Spira considered Dauphin's influence to have given Australian Bassets "soundness, better toplines, and eradicated obnoxious anatomical exaggerations having appeared in the breed." He thought another sire, Buchanan's American Dog, could have had equal impact, but few people were interested in using him as his stock was so very different to what they were used to.

By 1963 a number of Basset shows had been held, in conjunction with other sporting breed clubs. The 1963 Championship Show staged by the Basset Hound Club of New South Wales is notable for being the first 'stand alone' single breed Basset Hound show.

There are three Basset Hound clubs affiliated to the Australian National Kennel Council – The Basset Hound Club of New South Wales, the Basset Hound Club of

Victoria, and the Basset Hound Club of Queensland.

NEW ZEALAND

The Basset Hound Club was established in Auckland, New Zealand, in 1962. At that time, a Basset bitch named Lyndhaze Limmerck was imported from Australia into Christchurch by Eileen Slade and David Fiefield. She was bred by Hazel and Bill O'Hehir of the Lyndhaze kennels in Australia. She won two Best Puppy in Show titles and was the first Basset bitch to win a major prize in New Zealand. In Auckland, Mr and Mrs Hays' bitch, Tartarin Danielle (Mimi), won Best Puppy in Show at the Auckland Kennel Centre (now the Auckland Kennel Council) and Bassets were on the map in New Zealand as they were both given considerable publicity.

EUROPE

Northern Irish breed clubs are either affiliated to the Kennel Club in London or to the Irish Kennel Club, which is, in turn, a member of the FCI (Fédération Cynologique Internationale). The Basset Hound Club of Northern Ireland however is under the auspices of the KC.

The majority of European countries have their own Basset Hound clubs, licensed under the kennel club of their own country, which are mostly members of the FCI based in Belgium.

THE BASSET HOUND IN SWITZERLAND

It must not be forgotten that Bassets are popular in other countries too. Many of these, including

FCI/International, USA, Swiss, Luxembourg and Croatian Ch. Bellecombe No No Nanette. Owned by Grace Servais.

Switzerland, are member of the FCI. Some FCI countries have their own breeding regulations set by their national kennel club; other countries have none. Those of the Basset Hound Club of Switzerland (BHCS) are particularly stringent. A Basset cannot be used for breeding if it has not passed the Breeding Selection, consisting of two separate examinations – one of conformation and one of temperament, with a judge for each. In addition, the dog must have been X-rayed for hip and elbow dysplasia and received an eye examination (gonioscopy), the results of which will affect the conditions under which the Basset is allowed to be bred (if at all). There is also a list of faults, any of which will disqualify a Basset from being used for breeding. These selection and testing procedures are time-consuming and expensive, and unsurprisingly there are only

two active Basset Hound breeders in the country.

To show Bassets, FCI rules apply. To become an International (FCI) Champion a dog must win four CACIBs (Certificat d'aptitude au championnat/international de beauté) or 2 CACIBs and a Working Certificate, depending on the country. National championships demand a varying number of CACs (Certificat d'aptitude au championnat), also depending on the country (Switzerland requires four). In all cases there must be a year and a day between the first and last CACIB or CAC.

The Basset Hound "FCI Standard Number 163" will eventually be brought in line with the new Standard adopted by the country of origins of the breed (i.e. the UK). It will be applied by all FCI member countries. Further information can be found on the FCI's website.

A BASSET FOR YOUR LIFESTYLE

Chapter 3

There are usually three different types of people who become proud owners of a Basset Hound:

Those who do their homework by finding out all they can about the breed, which is highly recommended. Then, armed with the necessary information from having read all of the books and researched the internet, they find a reputable breeder.

There are the people who want a Basset Hound puppy almost immediately, or they may have considered it for some time but have done little or no research. Inevitably, and sadly, such people usually end up going to the wrong place or to the wrong people for a puppy, as they are the only ones who have puppies available most of the time.

The third kind are those who 'fall' into owning a Basset purely by accident, by taking on an unwanted family pet, perhaps from within their own family or from a friend or even a complete stranger. Someone who is willing to unselfishly adopt a dog, which says so much about their nature and character, is a very special person indeed.

Trying to avoid the wrong kind of breeder and establishment can be a minefield to the uninitiated.

POINTS TO CONSIDER

Before embarking on Basset ownership – whether you are planning to buy a puppy or rehome an adult – you must weigh up the pros and cons and decide if you can offer a suitable home.

TIME

Do you have sufficient time for a Basset Hound?

A young puppy initially needs four meals a day. He must go outside regularly for toileting purposes (if you want a house-clean dog), and he also needs your companionship.

A young couple who are both out at full-time work will not necessarily offer an attractive home, as far as a responsible breeder is concerned. A puppy will not thrive if he is left for long periods on his own, and although the breeder does not want to invade people's privacy, there may be doubts about the permanence of the relationship. A lot of dogs need rehoming because a relationship fails – both with married and unmarried couples.

A married couple may appear to offer a stable home, but if both people are working full-time, it is not an ideal situation, unless

Is the whole family
committed to
owning a Basset?

other family members are
prepared to puppy-sit during the
day.

The other options are:

- Doggy day care: You may be
able to find someone who
specialises in providing care for
daily boarders. This can work
quite well with a fully grown
dog but is not advisable with a
puppy, unless the facility is run
by people who understand the
unique growth pattern of dwarf
dogs and puppies (see Chapter
Five: The Best of Care).

- Dog sitter: You could employ
someone to come into your
home to look after your dog,
though you must consider if
you would want a stranger in
your home. Plus, what is the
point of paying a lot of money
for your dog, only to have him
give his allegiance to someone
else who walks him, talks to
him, plays with him, and
probably feeds him, too?

- Dog walker: This is good for an
older dog, but a puppy's
exercise needs to be carefully
monitored until he is mature –
about a year old – and you

would require a very caring
and careful person to ensure
that your puppy is not walked
too far, not walked on the
wrong surface and not walked
on a lead alongside a pack of
other dogs who are in the care
of the dog walker.

These options are worth
considering, but bear in mind
that it is not an ideal upbringing
for a puppy and may not result
in the well-adjusted, house-
trained adult you were hoping
for.

SPECIAL NEEDS

There are a number of specific issues with regard to your choice of a Basset Hound, which should be considered.

The Basset is a big dog on short legs; he is slow to mature – both in mind and body – but he has a very keen intelligence, which he frequently uses to his own advantage.

As a dwarf breed, the Basset will need special care during the growing period (see Chapter Five: the Best of Care). A Basset Hound can be quite long-lived – and the more care taken by you during his first year, the more likely he is to remain active and pain-free in later life.

Like most dogs in the hound group, a Basset is a pack animal and needs companionship; he is happiest when he is with the others in his pack. He will count his human family – and any other pets – as his pack, and this is one of the reasons why he so enjoys holiday times when his pack are all together and he can be content. But, as with any pack, there has to be firm leadership.

It must be stressed that the Basset Hound is a scent hound – he tracks the prey by its scent, just like a Bloodhound. Once he finds an interesting scent, he will want to follow it, and unless you have established good control of him, he will be deaf to all calls.

See Chapter Six: Training and Socialisation for advice on recall training.

In some occupations it may be possible to take a Basset to work, and most responsible breeders will have no objection to letting a Basset Hound go to a home where this is arranged.

MONEY

Can you afford to keep a Basset Hound?

The cost of feeding one dog tends to get absorbed in the weekly housekeeping budget, though if you purchase large sacks (15 kilos) of commercially prepared kibble (complete diet),

it will make a dent in your pocket.

Heath care also has to be paid for – you will need to budget for routine preventative care, as well as health problems as they occur – and the unexpected emergency. Pet insurance is advisable and can be paid as a monthly standing order.

Hidden costs involved in owning a Basset include extra washing powder (non-bio) and an extra run of the washing machine to wash dog blankets, bedding, towels and toys.

YOUR AGE AND HEALTH

Can older people, or those with disabilities, look after a Basset?

Provided the owner has a strong will and can train a Basset puppy into 'instant' obedience with a word (or a look), then age and disability can be managed - as it can be with the ownership of most breeds. Even the most exuberant Basset can be quite gentle and will adapt to his owner's disability. However, it is important that there is 24-hour back-up from other family members in this situation. It has

It is a bonus if you can take your Basset on holiday with you.

been found that a well-trained, well-socialised Basset can make an ideal partner for an autistic child.

COMMITMENT

Are you, and your family, committed to caring for a Basset Hound for the duration of his life?

The children want a puppy – but it usually ends up that mother has to feed him, toilet train him, train and exercise him. Children will say they will do all this – and will do at first – but will it last? Older children studying for school exams will be busy; young adults will probably be at college or university.

The husband wants a dog – but unless he is able to take the dog to work with him, it is usually the wife who ends up caring for him. *The wife/mother wants a dog* – she already expects to look after him, and she may be at home more of the time to enjoy his company.

Before embarking on Basset ownership, make sure the family is united in wanting a dog – and the primary carer is happy to take on the responsibility.

HOLIDAYS

What will you do with your Basset when you go on holiday?

Basset Hounds enjoy going away with their family on holiday,

particularly on a camping or caravanning trip. With the pet passport scheme, some British and European Basset Hounds can even join in with family holidays abroad.

If your family holiday is such that you are unable to take your Basset, it will be necessary to make arrangements for his care while you are away. Sometimes family members will be prepared to take care of your hound but, in most cases, you will have to place him in a boarding kennel. Not all boarding kennels cope easily with a noisy Basset Hound. This is a dog with a loud, resonant bark, and if he howls – a Basset speciality – he may set the rest of the dogs howling, too.

It would be wise to visit a number of kennels before making a decision regarding which is best suited to caring for your Basset. Check with the proprietor that your Basset can have his own crate and some of his own bedding, along with one or two of his favourite toys, which will help him to settle. A sudden change of diet may cause digestive problems, so ask if you can provide your Basset's food for the duration of his stay. Very few boarding kennels will refuse, and most will reduce the boarding fees accordingly.

FINDING A BASSET PUPPY

You have now decided that you and your family want to take on a Basset puppy. The next step is to find a responsible breeder who has a reputation for producing sound, healthy puppies that are typical of the breed.

The first point of contact should be with a breed club. This should be when you are starting to think of becoming the owner of a Basset, not afterwards when you have run into trouble. Sadly, many people who own Bassets only learn about the breed clubs – and their great value – when something goes wrong.

Breed clubs have contact details of breeders in your area, and these people will abide by the club's code of ethics. This is some form of guarantee showing that the breeder is working to a high standard, with the health and welfare of the breed as a top priority. You should also be told that it is far better to put your name on a waiting list belonging to a reputable breeder, and wait for that well-bred, even-tempered puppy.

An unsuspecting purchaser wanting an instant Basset can be easy prey for the person who has excess litters or has access to puppies from other so-called 'breeders'. It is a well-known fact that, once a puppy has been seen in one of these establishments, most kind-heated people are very reluctant to leave a poor little puppy in such a place.

A responsible breeder will never sell puppies younger than eight weeks old, and will only sell puppies and adults to homes where there is a reasonable expectation of a happy and healthy life. Breeders abiding by a code of ethics will also be prepared to help with the rehousing of a hound if the initial circumstances change.

Unfortunately, not all breeders will give you this back-up; with some you pay your money and are left to take your chances as they disappear into the sunset, often leaving little or no trace of their whereabouts.

Take time to find a breeder with a reputation for producing sound, healthy puppies that are typical of the breed.

If you go to a Championship show, you will be able to see a wide variety of Basset Hounds.

Whichever way you end up with your Basset – puppy or adult, planned or unplanned – in the blink of an eye you can suddenly feel totally out of your depth, even if you have owned dogs for many years. The task can seem very daunting because a Basset Hound does not fit into the same box as any other sort of dog and whatever dog knowledge you think you have, it all seems to leave immediately via the nearest exit!

Questions like, "What do I know about a Basset Hound?" and, "What have I let myself in for?" soon spring to mind. It's a road that is well worn and where many people have been before you.

This is where a good relationship with the puppy's breeder or welfare representative, if you are taking on a rescue Basset, is invaluable. It gives you a fall back that you can tap into. It is always there and always consistent. A true, caring breeder wants you to remain in touch, even if only for occasional updates and photos to show how the puppy is progressing. This is very important to the vast majority of breeders – keeping in touch and knowing their pups are doing well in loving homes is a primary concern. A responsible breeder is always there to help you should the need ever arise, no matter how big or small the problem appears to be. Welfare representatives also like to be updated from time to time, although they do tend to have many more contacts than the usual breeder.

RESEARCHING THE OPTIONS

Many breed clubs produce an annual newsletter or yearbook, which feature breeders' advertisements and photographs of their hounds. It is a good starting point to purchase the current (and possibly the previous) year's issue, just to see which hounds you like the best.

Basset Hounds can look very slightly different to each other, in the same way as members of one human family can look different from members of another family. Before purchasing a puppy, it is always wise, if possible, to see a number of different adults from different breeding kennels. The easiest way to do this is to go to a Basset Hound breed club event or attend a Championship Show if there is one not too far away from your home. Your national kennel club will provide contacts regarding such events. There will be subtle differences in kennel type, and some 'types' may be more to your taste than others. It is also worth talking to a number of owners to find out the full advantages – and disadvantages – of living with a Basset Hound before plunging in at the deep end!

It is important to see the puppies with their mother.

Do your research well and try not to be impatient. Use the internet as a tool, by all means, but use it with care. There are more 'puppy mills' puppy 'farmers' and 'cash-crop' breeders making a very good, tax-free living from internet puppy sales than there are caring breeders. If you are invited to see a breeder's Basset Hounds when they do *not* have puppies for sale, then it is well worth the journey and with no obligation on either side.

Never pay a deposit until you have actually chosen a puppy; a reputable breeder will not ask for one. Circumstances may change for one party or the other, or you may feel obliged to take a puppy you do not want after all.

VIEWING A LITTER

Where have the puppies been reared? In a draughty shed in the garden, in a purpose-built pen in the house, or a specially built clean, dry and warm kennel? Puppies brought up in a safe and warm environment mature better both in body and mind.

A purpose-built whelping area, which can easily be kept warm, dry and clean at all times, reduces the chances of illness/infection for mother and young. A large pen in the house ensures that the puppies are used to household noises, such as the vacuum cleaner, television – and people. A puppy brought up in a large playpen area in the working/busy room of the house is far better socialised than one brought up in a garden shed.

Puppies whelped and brought up with a free run of the house or shed and garden will certainly have learned how to cause damage by chewing and may easily have suffered some damage to themselves before being sold – by pulling or knocking objects over, by jumping on and off furniture, and, perhaps, up and down steps at a time when their growth plates are most vulnerable to injury.

Some breeders will allow visits to see the puppies from about two weeks old, provided you guarantee to wear fresh, clean, 'old' clothes and are prepared to leave your footwear in the entrance. The 'old clothes' are because you can expect to be sprayed with a special disinfectant. The breeder will go through the same regime themselves, after trips outside the home to minimise the risk of infection.

Look closely at the puppies. Do they appear dull and lethargic, or are they boisterous and lively, playing rough games with their siblings? Do they come forward to greet you with interest or do they lie listlessly on their bed? Do they have shiny or dull coats? Look at the puppies' feet: have their nails been trimmed? As puppies nurse, they 'paddle' their feet against the bitch – imagine the pain they would inflict if they had long nails. Look for telltale scratches on the bitch's underside.

Use your nose – does the puppy have smelly ears? If good husbandry and basic health care has been observed, the ears should be clean and free from odour. Both the bitch and the puppies should have healthy, shiny coats, bright, clear eyes and cold, moist noses – runny eyes and hot, dry or runny noses indicate potential health problems.

THE PARENTS

"Always see the puppies' mother" is good advice. But it is amazing how many people do not heed it. However, seeing the mother is a good gauge of the care that has gone into rearing the litter. Puppies tend to 'pull a bitch down', but one that has been well cared for and correctly fed will still have plenty of flesh covering her ribs. She will still carry a reasonably dense, sleek and healthy coat, and she should be bright-eyed, outgoing and sociable.

Look at the bitch's toenails. While nursing her litter she will not have had much in the way of exercise, but a caring breeder will have kept her nails short and her feet comfortable.

In most cases it is not possible to see the father of the puppies, unless it is a very large show kennel that has a number of show dogs on the premises. However, puppy farmers, puppy mills and cash-crop breeders may also have a male Basset who is used to sire *all* the puppies that are bred on the premises, so beware.

If you are able to see the sire, try to assess his general state of health and his temperament.

The breeder will help you to assess a puppy to see if he has show potential.

Resist the temptation of taking on two puppies from the same litter.

Does he appear outgoing and friendly? Is his coat dense, clean and gleaming? Have his nails been trimmed? You also need to assess breed points – for example, his length of body should come from the length of his ribcage and with a short waist, which is good? If he has a long distance from the end of his ribs to his pelvis it is not so good as it can give a weakness to the back.

For more information on conformation, see Chapter Seven: The Perfect Basset.

In the majority of cases, the father of the puppies will belong to another kennel, though the breeder should be able to show you a photograph and a pedigree, and give details of his show record.

If you have sourced your puppy via a breed club, you may have been advised of a show or social/fun event you could attend

in order meet the breeders, and you may also have the opportunity to see the sire before going to view the litter.

CHOOSING A PUPPY

If you purchase from a show kennel, do not expect to have the pick of the litter. In most cases, the breeder has produced a litter in order to have the pick of the litter themselves so they can bring out something new to show. However, when you look at the puppies in a good-quality show-bred litter, it is very doubtful that you will see any difference between them; they have all been carefully bred for good health and conformation. A breeder who shows in beauty competitions will explain why they prefer one puppy against the other, focusing on the finer points, and you will wonder what all the fuss is about! But not all show-bred dogs are potential

show winners.

A show breeder will retain the 'best' for himself and will often run on more than one puppy, of either or both sexes, to see how they develop. Quite often a run-on puppy can be purchased at four to six months from a show breeder. There is nothing wrong with the pup - he may have a very minor fault that means he may not make the grade in the show ring. A puppy of this type may cost the same as an eight-week-old puppy or he might cost a little more. However, this is often a good deal, as the puppy will be on fewer meals a day, he will be fully inoculated, and, if you are lucky, he may be house-trained.

If you do decide to show your Basset Hound, the show breeder will ensure that you have puppy with potential. This is in the breeder's own interest, as they will only want good-quality stock

BREEDING TERMS

Never agree to take a bitch puppy on breeding terms. This is a signed agreement, stipulating that the new owner will mate the bitch to a dog of the breeder's choice (and, possibly, pay the stud fee). The breeder then has the pick of the litter.

In essence, the bitch owner will pay the price of the original puppy three times - i.e. the purchase price, the stud fee and the rearing of a puppy. Furthermore, never agree to pay a stud fee and also give a puppy 'back' to the stud dog owner.

Quite apart from ending up out of pocket, breeding a litter is very hard work for an experienced breeder; it is even harder work for an inexperienced breeder – and with complications that may arise, you might not only lose the litter, but the bitch, too.

exhibited in the ring with their affix. The breeder will explain what the judge is looking for and will demonstrate the good points to bring forward, as well as showing you how to minimise the slightly less good points. Advice will also be given about the subtle changes to expect in conformation as the puppy matures, and how to raise your puppy to make sure that he fulfils his potential.

MALE OR FEMALE?
It really doesn't matter – there is not a lot of difference in temperament (see Chapter One). If you intend to neuter your Basset on maturity, you are far better to choose the puppy who chooses you – regardless of its sex.

COLOURS AND MARKINGS
Colours and markings are not important, as there is no set colour or pattern within the requirements of the Breed Standard (see Chapter Seven: The Perfect Basset). The puppy who chooses you will be the ideal colour and have the most perfect markings…

MORE THAN ONE?
Most people who start off with one Basset soon want another! Bassets enjoy the company of people and other breeds of dog, but, best of all, they enjoy the company of another Basset Hound. If you decide you do want to have two Bassets as companions for each other, purchase them singly. Never be

persuaded to purchase two puppies from the same litter or of the same age. It results in twice as much work, lengthens the period of toilet-training, and one puppy may well dominate the other. When away from home, the dominant puppy can often be nervous, whilst the bullied puppy may become more confident. The only winner in this scenario will be the breeder who will be delighted to have made two sales!

Taking on two Bassets at the same time is a big cause of rehoming – two dogs can be too much to cope with, particularly if they are not properly trained in the early stages. Both dogs need one-on-one training, which is virtually impossible to provide unless you are very dedicated.

If you decide to take on another Basset, wait until your first puppy is at least 12 months of age. By this time he will be fully house-trained and will have learnt basic good manners, which he may pass on to the new baby. You will have to ensure that the older dog does not play too exuberantly with the puppy, and it would be wise to purchase another crate specifically for the puppy to sleep in overnight, or when you go out, until he is about a year old. It is best – and safest – to have a puppy of the same sex as the older Basset, unless the older Basset has been neutered.

Taking on an older dog may be a better option for you.

TAKING ON AN OLDER DOG

For some, taking on an older Basset is the better option. Perhaps a puppy would not fit into the household whereas an adult just might. In some cases, a reputable breeder will have an older Basset of their own breeding that they would be willing to rehome with the right person. This could be a dog that has been retired from showing, or a brood bitch who has come to the end of her breeding career. If the right home comes along, the breeder will sell such a dog, at a very nominal price, to a home where the Basset can live as a very much-loved pet.

The other option is to take on a rescued dog. There are many Bassets who need rehoming through no fault of their own – family break-up, the arrival of a new baby, a change of job – are all common reasons why a dog is put up for adoption. In some cases, a Basset may need rehoming because he has become unruly in his own home due to lack of proper management and training. Such a dog can be retrained, but he will need to go to someone with the necessary experience.

If you are thinking of taking on an older Basset Hound, find out as much as possible about the dog in question before committing yourself.

SUMMING UP

The well-known saying from Dogs Trust – *A dog is for life not just for Christmas* – should be very seriously considered before getting *any* dog.

Adopting a dog is about as serious as adopting a child. Taking a Basset Hound into your home should be considered a lifetime responsibility. Inevitably, events change in our lives and we have to adapt, but we still have to consider our dogs. A Basset can adapt to different circumstances – just give him the chance.

THE NEW ARRIVAL

Now you have decided to bring a Basset Hound into your life, the next step is to prepare your home and garden for the new arrival. You need to create a safe environment for your puppy – and take certain precautions to keep the environment safe from your new pup. If you have children, they must also be taken into the equation.

IN THE GARDEN

Before you bring your new puppy home, examine your garden boundaries very carefully. It is amazing what a small space a puppy can squeeze through, so potential escape routes need to be found and blocked. A garden wall, provided it is not too low, is an ideal barrier, though you must ensure that there is nothing stored against the wall to supply an impromptu 'stair' to climb to the top of it.

If your garden is surrounded by hedges, you will need to be especially careful, as there can be lots of gaps to crawl through. The best plan is to secure wire netting along the base line of the hedge so your Basset puppy cannot find a way out. Remember, the Basset crawls through thick undergrowth in order to flush game to the guns. If the boundary is a fence, ensure that it is in good repair at the base and cannot be easily broken through.

If you have a gate leading from the garden, it must have a secure fastening. Ideally, you would have a gate with a spring, which will close itself if you forget. Make sure that the gate sits fairly close to the ground, with no puppy-sized gap underneath. Open-work gates, such as farm gates, should be covered with wire netting to ensure that the puppy cannot climb through.

A SAFE AREA

The best and safest solution is to allocate a fenced area of hard and soft ground outside the back door leading into the garden, which will give security for your Basset to rest and play, without supervision. Your Basset will enjoy 'helping' you in the garden but will be perfectly happy in his own little area. Within this area, you can designate a toilet area – it is much easier to keep a smaller area clean and hygienic than the whole garden.

VEGETABLES AND PLANTS

Some garden shrubs, bulbs and flowers are poisonous to dogs, as are some commercial products, like cocoa mulch, which is spread round plants to keep the weeds down. You will need to seek professional advice, either locally

Nothing is safe if you have a Basset....

Try to see your home from a puppy's perspective.

or on the internet, if you are not sure of the safety of the plants in your garden.

If you have a vegetable garden, it would be wise to make it Basset-proof – as these dogs are very adept at eating peas and beans off the vine, digging up carrots and potatoes, chewing cabbage and cauliflowers and uprooting lettuce. Though the pips and stones are not good for them, they will eat fallen apples, pears and plums – and are likely to be stung by wasps in the process. Bassets help themselves to soft fruit, too.

OTHER GARDEN HAZARDS

A pond or a swimming pool can be dangerous – even lethal – if an unsupervised puppy goes exploring. Fence them off so they are completely out of bounds – unless you are present to supervise your Basset while he has a swim.

A glass greenhouse will need some protection around the sides, and a garden shed can be dug under, particularly if you have burrowing rabbits in your garden. You will also need to make sure that the doors are well secured so an inquisitive puppy is barred.

STEPS

Many properties have a step or steps down from the house door into the yard or garden. The potential for growth-plate damage cannot be stressed enough, and an immature Basset should be prevented from using steps whenever possible. A wooden ramp to cover the steps, with sides to prevent the puppy jumping down sideways, can be used until the growth plates have closed. This will pay dividends for your Basset Hound's future health and longevity. There are no commercial ramps on the market for this purpose, but they are not difficult to build. The ramp must not be too steep, and it must be strong because the family will tread on it until the dog is fully grown. For more information on growth plates, see Chapter Five: The Best of Care.

IN THE HOME

Your Basset Hound will want to be with you and, surely, the reason for purchasing a Basset is because you wish to spend time with him. However, you must provide a safe environment for a young, inquisitive puppy.

A Basset Hound will consider that you never provide enough interesting toys and, consequently, he will have to find his own. This could include: an oven glove, a tea towel, or the television remote control – a Basset can be very inventive as regards toys. Consider electrical and telephone wires; they may dangle enticingly but are dangerous if chewed. Never leave your glasses and book on a low coffee table as they may look like toys – even to an adult Basset Hound. Ornaments on low tables or window ledges may be investigated, or knocked off by a wagging tail and broken. Children's toys are hugely attractive, but chewed toys spell heartbreak for children and can cause considerable problems if

pieces are swallowed by your puppy. There are far too many cases where veterinary intervention has been required to remove an obstruction, and, tragically, the consequences can be lethal.

Decide where your puppy is allowed free access in the house and where he is not allowed. A Basset should not go up and down stairs on a routine basis, as this will cause growth-plate damage. This means you will want to keep your Basset on the ground floor. You may also decide you want to restrict access to the kitchen, or you may want one Basset-free room, such as study, which may have a lot of electrical cables.

Think about the layout of your home and buy, or build, baby gates for the 'no go' areas, such as the bottom of the stairs and entrance to the kitchen.

Basset puppies 'explore' with their mouths and are very good at chewing special things, such as antique table legs or coffee table corners, but you will probably never catch your pup red-handed! You can purchase special aerosol sprays to prevent a puppy – or adult (yes, they chew too) – from returning to a partially chewed area.

BUYING EQUIPMENT

Just like any human baby, a new puppy is expensive – not just the initial cost of the puppy but everything else you will need to purchase before you bring your new 'baby' home.

A PLACE TO SLEEP

It is well worth considering buying a crate, sometimes referred to as an indoor kennel. It is an investment, but it will protect

A Basset will soon look on a crate as his own special den.

your home from puppy damage and it will last your Basset a lifetime. The breeder may have already been using a large crate for the mother and puppies to sleep in, so your pup may be accustomed to using one.

The minimum size of crate for an adult Basset Hound is 900 mm x 600 mm x 650 mm high (3 ft x 2 ft x 2 ft 3 inches.) Obviously, it will be too large for a puppy, but a cage is an ideal aid to toilet training. An adult-sized cage for a tiny puppy means that half the cage can be the bed area and the other half can be lined with newspaper for toilet purposes.

If possible, locate the crate in the room where you and your family spend most of the time – you can relax in your favourite chair and your Basset can relax in his bed. A bed in a barren utility room could be seen as banishment, and your Basset may be reluctant to use it except during the night – and he

may object to that, too.

A conservatory may seem like a good place to locate a crate, but bear in mind how hot it will get in the summer. It is not a good idea to site a crate in a conservatory permanently.

BEDDING

You will need bedding to put in the crate; the best type to buy is the type made of synthetic fleece. The theory is that moisture runs through the pile and out through the backing so a puppy will not be damp and uncomfortable if he wets the bedding. This type of bedding is machine-washable and easy to dry. However, the more it is washed, the less waterproof the backing becomes; nevertheless, it is absolutely ideal for a puppy who is learning about toilet training.

Non-biological washing powder, suitable for baby clothes, is recommended for washing bedding and towels, as the

brighteners in biological powders can cause irritation to tender parts of the skin.

BOWLS

Bassets do not just drink their water – they wash their mouths out and slobber in it too. You will therefore need a water bowl that stands up to heavy wear. Stone bowls are cumbersome to wash and heavy to put down when full of water, and they soon become cracked. Plastic bowls are not recommended; they are lightweight and so will move across the floor, and will be considered good 'toys'. The best type to buy are stainless-steel dishes, which can be easily washed and are virtually indestructible. Some have a rubber circle around the base, which stops the dish moving across the floor as the dog is eating or drinking.

COLLAR AND LEAD

For a puppy, the ideal collar and lead is in an integral piece. The collar is adjustable and this will enable it to 'grow' with the puppy. A leather collar will be too stiff and heavy at this stage. The dewlap (the loose, pendulous skin at the neck and throat) means the circumference of the neck of an adult tends to be wider than the head, so a collar can be easily slipped off. A leather collar that is tight enough not to slip off will, in a short space of time, chafe the dewlap, and there will be an enclosed sweaty area where yeast will grow, causing the Basset to

Synthetic fleece bedding is easy to wash and quick to dry.

scratch, irritating the skin even more.

If your Basset Hound is to wear a collar at all times, even in the home, then use a light (though strong) fabric collar. If your hound has the free run of your garden, including low shrubbery, be aware that the collar could catch in a low branch and your hound could be injured in trying to get free.

Your Basset Hound should have contact details attached to his collar. But if the worst happens and your dog escapes when he is not wearing a collar, you have little hope of finding him. For this reason, it is advisable to get a form of permanent ID; it is a relatively easy procedure to get your Basset tattooed or microchipped.

You will also need a strong lead, as an adult Basset is a powerful dog. Extending leads may be useful in the local park, but do make sure that the lead you use is strong enough to hold a 30-kilo dog – and that you are strong enough to hold on and maintain control. The further away the hound is on such a lead, the heavier he seems!

GROOMING ESSENTIALS
A puppy may have a slightly soft coat, but a well-reared pup should have been fed on a diet that retains the natural oils in the coat. All you will need to purchase with regard to coat care is a rubber hound glove, which will take any loose undercoat away. Brush your Basset Hound in the garden in the spring and enjoy watching the birds collect the hair for their nests.

Cleaning teeth with a human toothbrush is not practical with a puppy that is teething and may have sore gums. Soft brushes, which can be worn on your finger, are available – along with meat-flavoured toothpaste (found in most pet supermarkets). This type of brush gives more control, though a puppy who is teething will not be too keen on anything moving around his sore gums.

There are a number of good-quality nail clippers readily available. Bear in mind that nail clippers suitable for humans will not suit the round nails of a Basset Hound. The most appropriate are the guillotine claw clippers, made by a number of manufacturers and available in most pet supermarkets or via the internet.

For information on grooming, see Chapter Five: the Best of Care.

TOYS
Bassets love their toys – and there is a wide variety to choose from. Toys suitable for children are not suitable for dogs and it is recommended that all toys are purchased from a reputable pet store or internet distributor. Do not purchase toys with button eyes or noses, as these are the first things your Basset will try (successfully) to remove.

Soft toys may soon be disembowelled, though the remaining parts may survive as a favourite for some time. If it is a squeaky toy, do make sure the 'squeak' is removed to prevent your Basset swallowing it. All soft toys will need a periodic wash and can go in the washing machine with the bedding.

Tennis balls are a good size for a puppy, but an adult Basset Hound

A Basset puppy will enjoy any toys you provide – but make sure they are suitably robust.

needs a much larger ball that cannot stick in the throat. Larger, more solid and slightly ridged balls can be partially carried in the mouth, tossed in the air or kicked around and chased; some have chimes or rattles inside. There are a number of toys – mainly brightly coloured ropes with balls attached – which are made out of some type of rubbery material. The ball soon crumbles, helped along by the Basset's jaws, of course, but the coloured rope will last, being carried around for some time. Once you notice the ball disintegrating, it is best to remove it before your hound eats it.

Bassets are very clever at finding 'toys'. They can have a wonderful game with a cardboard box – it is your misfortune if it contained something important, such as screws or nails. Your Basset Hound may find an interesting piece of stick when out for a walk,

although he may not be prepared to carry it home. However, if you bring it home for him, it is still 'his' and he will get very upset if you put it on the fire.

Unless you are happy with your Basset's toys permanently scattered around the floor, you will need a toy box. A plastic washing-up bowl makes an ideal container – your Basset will be able to rummage around to find that special toy when it is needed.

PUPPY FOOD

A caring and reputable breeder will provide a sample of food to take away with your puppy, but do obtain a bag of the same food so you can continue the same feeding regime. If you are unable to purchase the brand easily, or locally, then a gradual change-over, by mixing the breeder's food with new food in ever-increasing quantities, will prevent an upset

stomach. If your water is particularly hard or soft, it may sometimes help if you take a large empty plastic bottle to bring home some of the water from the breeder's area. Give the puppy the water he is used to at first, then gradually mix your own with it.

For more information on feeding, see Chapter Five: The Best of Care.

FOR HOLIDAYS

If you go caravanning and use an awning, or go camping in a tent, you will find a crate is ideal for your Basset Hound's bedroom. You can also fasten wire-mesh panels to make a playpen so your Basset cannot stray.

If you are taking part in any activity that does warrant a certain amount of inattention from the owner – such as fishing – it is advisable to fasten a long rope to your Basset Hound's collar and fasten it to a stake so that he cannot wander off on an interesting scent. A tie-out stake is like an enormous corkscrew (about 20 cm or 8 ins long), which can be screwed quite deeply into the ground. There is a swivel clip at the top for attaching a dog lead, or a longer length of rope, which is then fastened to your Basset Hound's collar. Most dedicated pet stores sell these or they can be purchased via the internet.

FINDING A VET

It is advisable to ask dog owners who live in your locality which veterinary practice they recommend. Nobody minds

A tie-out stake is useful at times when you cannot fully supervise your dog.

being accosted in the street if you are admiring their dog and asking their advice! Visit the local practices that have been recommended and see which one appears most suitable. Remember, it is not just about convenience; it is far more important to find out if the vets have experience with treating Basset Hounds.

Talk to the receptionist or veterinary nurse and find out what happens if you have an emergency in the middle of the night. Some practices are able to deal with an out-of-hours emergency, but others refer you to another specialist emergency practice, which may be quite some distance away – and could be expensive.

In some cases, puppies will have had their first inoculation before they go to their new homes. Most practices will be happy to give the second inoculation, but a few will insist on starting the whole inoculation procedure again, which is expensive and puts undue stress on a young puppy. If the veterinary practice in question pursues this policy, it would be wise to contact the breeder and make sure your pup is not vaccinated prior to collection.

If you have any doubts about the health of your Basset, it is important to seek expert advice and help as soon as a problem occurs. This is one of the reasons

At last the time has come to collect your Basset puppy.

why you need to source a good veterinary practice before you bring your puppy home. You should also keep in touch with your puppy's breeder, who will be interested to know how their stock is faring and can often help with advice in the early stages of any problem to prevent it worsening.

COLLECTING YOUR PUPPY
Never agree to take a puppy that is less than seven and a half weeks old, which is still rather early. Eight weeks is the ideal time. By this stage, the mother will have taught the pups some manners and you will be able to see the puppies at their best stage of growth. The next 'all-together' stage of growth is about 12 weeks – then the puppy becomes like a

lanky teenager until six months of age when he starts to 'come together' and looks more like the finished young adult.

Never agree to pick up your puppy at a motorway services – or any other agreed meeting point – no matter how many times you have enjoyed speaking to the breeder over the telephone. If you intend the puppy to be a surprise present, make the surprise part of it a visit to a pet store in order to choose the puppy's toys, feeding and water bowls and other equipment.

Make sure that you have prepared your vehicle for the journey to collect your puppy. If your car is large enough to allow the crate to be put up, then this is ideal for travelling with the puppy. Otherwise it is best if you do not go alone. A companion sitting in the back seat, which is suitably covered with newspaper and a bedding, will be able to care for the puppy and ensure that he travels safely to your home. Take some extra bedding, plenty of newspaper/kitchen roll, some 'poo bags' or nappy bags, and a water bowl – the breeder can supply you with water if you have a long journey. It is unlikely that your pup will want to eat, and this is not really recommended for such a journey. Your puppy will come to no harm if he misses a meal during the traveling time.

Hopefully, you will have already

visited the breeder's premises on a previous occasion, to view the litter, and will have arranged the day and time for collecting your puppy. However, it would be a courtesy to phone just as you are about to leave home and give an estimated time of arrival. If you have to travel some distance, make sure you eat before you pick up your puppy so that he is not left unattended in the car on the journey home.

Take a collar and lead, but unless your puppy is older and has been fully inoculated, do not take him out of the car to walk on ground where other dogs may have roamed.

THE PAPERWORK

There is a lot of paperwork involved in acquiring a puppy. You will be given a copy of the pedigree and the Kennel Club registration documents.

Some breeders will have a veterinary surgeon visit in order to give the puppies a first inoculation before they leave the premises. If this is the case, you will be given a certificate signed by the vet who carried out the procedure and who would, at the same time, have checked the health of the puppy.

Many breeders also insure their puppies for the first few weeks in the new home – this is usually done by a phone call just before you leave – and you may consider it is worth continuing the insurance.

You will be given a feeding guide and details of worming and flea treatments to date, as well as a list of dos and don'ts regarding the care of your puppy. Read this carefully; it will contain a lot of invaluable information.

ARRIVING HOME

As soon as your puppy arrives in his new home, he will be the centre of attention and everyone in the family will want to pet and cuddle him – but first things first. Take your pup to the area you have designated as his toilet area. Let him relieve himself if he will, and give him lots of praise if he obliges. Do not rush your puppy; let him explore the areas where he is to have free access.

Leave a treat on the bed inside his new crate. A puppy who is already used to a crate may not need tempting into it, but a puppy who has never seen a crate before needs to go in voluntarily at first. Until your puppy is used to his new surroundings, he should not be picked up or played with by strangers – and this includes other family members and friends!

Children can become very excitable and fractious when they are tired, and it is just the same with a Basset puppy. Consequently, he should be left to explore and find his own way around, in his own time. Friends and neighbours can be invited to meet him a few days later when he feels more secure in his new home.

When he has explored and sniffed, he will enjoy a gentle stroke and cuddle. Looking to the future, is it far better for you to sit on the floor to do this rather than allowing your Basset on to your lap or on the furniture. A fully-grown Basset Hound is a heavy dog and, once allowed on the furniture – even via your lap – he

Give your puppy a chance to explore his new surroundings.

will consider that this is where he should be. A Basset can be stubborn as well as heavy, so trying to get him off a comfortable chair will become a battle of wills. This is a battle that you might succeed with, but one that other family members will have great difficulty in winning. An upturned stool on your favourite chair or a dining chair laid across the sofa are usually good deterrents – but when you go out and leave your Basset Hound alone for a while, it is far safer to put him to bed in his crate and close the door, as you would at night time.

Your Basset puppy will look unbelievably sweet, but do not make the mistake of constantly picking him up and carrying him, or sitting him on your lap for cuddles. When he becomes too heavy, he will not understand why you are no longer keen on the idea. If his friendly overtures are met with rejection and cross words, he will feel bewildered and unloved.

INTRODUCING CHILDREN

Bassets and children can be the best of friends, but you must establish some important rules so relations get off to a good start.

Children will be very excited when a new puppy comes home, but you must try to keep everything as calm as possible and supervise all interactions. Do not let a small child pick up the puppy. A 10-week-old puppy is very heavy and very wriggly, and can be dropped all too easily. This could result in broken limbs or growth-plate damage to the legs.

A Basset will soon form a special relationship with children in the family.

Encourage your children to sit on the floor when playing with the puppy and this type of accident will be avoided.

Children must be taught that the puppy's bed or crate is sacrosanct; a Basset Hound will quite happily share – but if he is in a deep sleep, any interloper into his area could possibly trigger an automatic defence reaction before he is fully awake. Sometimes a dog needs a safe place to get away from an over-exuberant and pushy young child.

A child should also be taught never to interfere with a puppy – or an adult – while he is eating. Teasing in any form – with food or with toys – is also banned. If an animal of any kind is teased, it will make him frustrated and angry. A child will lash out and hit or kick another child who is teasing him or her, but a dog uses his mouth and will bite. Do not allow a child to tease the puppy into becoming frustrated, as this teaches a puppy

to be aggressive. A really frustrated adult dog (of any breed) can become angry and, in such a case, he is dangerous.

PLAY BITING

In the nest, puppies mouth and bite each other, and so it is natural for them to continue this behaviour and direct it at people when they first leave their litter. It is often children who get the worst of this, which can cause problems.

It is important to understand that the Basset is a hound with the very basic instinct to catch live prey, which squeals in fear and wriggles to escape. The natural instinct of a hound is to grip the prey tighter to prevent its escape. Therefore, training a hound not to bite and grip is slightly different to the training for other breeds.

A hand that is quickly snatched away is liable to be badly scratched. Should a puppy try to play-bite a child, the child should be taught to very gently grasp the lower jaw and tell the dog: "No biting". The dog is so amazed, he stops biting, and very soon learns that this action is not acceptable.

MEETING THE RESIDENT DOG

If you already have a dog, take him with you when you collect your puppy. Let him meet the puppy on neutral ground before you put them both in the car. Do not travel the puppy in the same section as the older dog on this first occasion.

When you arrive home, let the older dog, on his lead, escort the puppy into the garden. The older dog may get a little boisterous, so speak to him calmly and allow the two dogs to get to know each other without too much interference. Try to ensure that the older dog does not get too exuberant or that the puppy does not become over-excited.

When the older dog has got over the novelty of meeting the pup, allow them both into the house. The two will soon establish their own relationship, but do not leave them alone together until you are confident that the puppy has been fully accepted.

CAT FRIENDLY

If you have a cat, allow the cat and puppy to meet in the garden, making sure the pup does not have the opportunity to chase. Then take them both into the house together. The cat will walk away with a stiff, haughty gait, and it is unlikely that there will ever be much interaction between the two from thereon. Some cats and Basset Hounds do get on remarkably well. It is up to the cat!

THE FIRST NIGHT

The crate should already have been prepared before you collected your puppy. Cover the bottom tray with plenty of newspaper, but not so much that the tray is full and will not slide out of the removal slot at the bottom. Put the bedding in the back half of the crate. You can buy a small water bowl to clip on the side of a crate. This should be placed not too high up and be at the front end of the crate, which is covered with newspaper. When the puppy is not in his crate, you can keep the door open with an elastic bungee, but this should be removed once the puppy is in the crate, as the hook is rather tempting to chew. If the puppy has been used to a crate, he will wander in and sleep quite soon after his meal.

Well before you go to bed, play with your puppy until he is tired – then play with him some more until he really would like you to go away to allow him to go to sleep. Give him the word of command for bedtime and put him into the cage and leave him straight away. He will be glad to see you go! He will wake during the early hours of the morning and whimper - but you must forbid everybody in the family (including yourself) from going downstairs to him, or crying will become a regular habit and will graduate from a whimper to a loud howl. It may be as well to warn the neighbours that the first two or three nights might be a little noisy.

If you have another dog – or a cat – placing their bed close to the puppy crate will give some comfort. A puppy who is used to sleeping in the crate during the night will be quite happy shut in for a part of the day, if you have to go out for any reason. Continue to make sure the puppy is very tired before being shut into the crate for the first two or three nights.

Your puppy will miss the company of his littermates for the first few nights.

HOUSE-TRAINING

Teaching your Basset puppy to be clean in the house is a top priority and should be started from day one.

As discussed, it is a good idea to allocate a toilet area in the garden and always take him out to this spot to relieve himself. It also helps if you have a verbal cue that the puppy will associate with the appropriate response. We have noticed that our automatic cry of "Out, out, quick, quick" as the puppy is taken outside for toilet purposes has remained as a 'toilet call' for the adults. We also have a reward call of "Yeah", and this is still appreciated by the adults who sometimes come and tell us that they have been good, and ask for a "Yeah"!

Keep a supply of poo bags or nappy bags handy for cleaning up immediately afterwards.

Establishing a routine and taking your puppy out at regular intervals is a great aid to house-training. Your pup will need to go out at the following times:
- First thing in the morning
- After mealtimes
- After a play session
- On waking from a nap
- Last thing at night.

In the first weeks, a puppy should be given the opportunity to relieve himself every two hours as a minimum requirement. The more often your puppy gets it 'right', the quicker he will learn.

Puppies need a lot of sleep. Put a drowsy puppy in the crate frequently during the day, and, when he wakes up, take him

Establish a routine of taking your pup out at regular intervals.

outside using your verbal cue. Use your reward word afterwards and you will soon have a clean Basset.

WHEN ACCIDENTS HAPPEN

It is inevitable that neither you, nor your Basset, will always get the timing right and there will be accidents in the house. The worst thing you can do is shout at the puppy and rub his nose in the mess. Instead, take him out to his normal toilet area.

Do try to keep half an eye on your puppy at all times. His behaviour will change slightly when he is looking for a suitable 'spot'. He may scurry a little or go round in circles, or he may even go towards the door and look up at it, expecting it to miraculously open – this is progress!

HANDLING

Regular grooming, nail clipping, ear cleaning and tooth care will

teach your Basset to be used to being handled by yourself and your family. But it is important that your Basset is accustomed to being handled by others, such as the vet or kennel staff if he is to board whilst you are away.

Whether or not you have any intention of showing your puppy, ringcraft classes are useful in this respect. At a conformation show, the judge will give your dog a thorough hands-on examination, and ringcraft training will ensure that your Basset is used to other people touching him without him being afraid. Your breeder or breed club will be able to advise where to find a local class.

EXERCISE

Until your puppy has been fully inoculated, he must not be taken to public areas where other dogs or urban foxes will have been. For the first few weeks, your puppy will be gaining sufficient exercise

HANDLING

A puppy needs to be accustomed to all over handling so that he will accept being groomed and, when necessary, examined by a vet.

Stroke your Basset along the length of his back...

...reaching down to the tip of the tail.

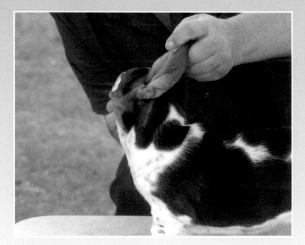

Check the ears.

Part the lips and examine the teeth and gums.

in his fenced garden area. Once fully inoculated he can go out on a lead for very short walks on a 'hard' area, such as the footpath, or slightly longer walks on a 'soft' area, such as grass or sandy beach. Do not let him off the lead to run and jump and shout with other, bigger dogs. The risk of growth-plate damage is too high (see Chapter 5).

REHOMING A BASSET

Basset Hounds are quite pragmatic and will settle into a new home quite quickly. Unfortunately, they may also come with a lot of unwanted bad habits – such as sleeping on the furniture or toileting in the house – because the first owners did not train them in a consistent manner. A Basset is essentially a pack hound and, in the manner of a pack, expects the strongest of the pack to be the pack leader. If the rest of the pack is weak, he will attempt to take control, so you must be strong.

In such a case, it would be wise to go back to basics. Take the hound out to toilet at very regular intervals, using your command word, praise word and, perhaps, a treat on successful completion. If the dog attempts to get up on to the furniture, clap your hands loudly to distract him, tell him to get down, and call him to you. When he obeys, give him a treat. Until he learns that the furniture is out of bounds, it may be wise to make it difficult for him to get on to it by placing an obstacle, such as a dining chair or large stool, in the way.

An adult Basset that is unused to a crate will, at first, need a bribe to encourage him to go into the crate and settle. Try giving him a toy filled with food treats. It will take him some to get the treats out, which will keep him well occupied.

A rehomed Basset will never forget his old life but, given time, he will settle in a new home. Keep him busy with new training exercises (see Chapter Six: Training and Socialisation) so that his mind is fully occupied and he looks on you as a fun person to be with.

Never rehome a Basset if you do not intend keeping him with you for the rest of his life.

If you are rehoming a Basset, you will need to give him time to adjust to his change of circumstance.

THE BEST OF CARE

When you first consider bringing a puppy or adult dog into your home, think long and hard about making such a commitment. The duty and responsibility of bringing up a dog is just like the duty and responsibility of bringing up a child. Both need to learn about toilet training, to be fed the correct diet, to be taught what is acceptable behaviour and what is not – and both need unconditional affection. In the early days it requires effort from you, but the returns are definitely worth it. The commitment you make will be well repaid throughout your Basset's life.

DIET AND NUTRITION

A dog is an omnivore, the same as humans. Just like us, a dog needs a balanced diet containing all the essential nutrients. We enjoy a varied diet, but most dogs are perfectly happy to eat the same food, which will generally be a commercially produced diet.

There are many brands of good-quality dog food available from many outlets. Generally speaking, puppies require a higher protein level than adults. Do remember, however, that too much protein will not only cost you more money, it could also damage a dog's long-term health. This, in turn, could lead to increased vet bills.

Many owners opt for a complete diet, which is convenient and easy to feed. Different diets are formulated depending on your dog's age and lifestyle, and there are even prescription diets for dogs with specific health issues, as well as diets for dogs suffering from allergies. Remember, if you wish to feed a complete diet, no meat should be added at all. If you wish to feed the adult dog meat and mixer only, then give one-third cooked or canned meat to two-thirds mixer – by volume, not weight.

Contrary to popular belief, large amounts of meat are not good for your dog. A dog fed on an excess of protein (levels vary for different dogs) may become hyperactive. If this happens, reduce the meat and increase the biscuit.

If you are feeding commercially prepared food, it is important to check the constituents of the food for colouring and permitted additives, some of which can have a tendency to make a Basset hyperactive (in the same way that certain commercially manufactured foods and drinks can affect children). Be aware that some commercially produced dog 'treats' may also have the same

65

The aim is to feed a well-balanced diet that is suited to your Basset's age and lifestyle.

oranges will be enjoyed, and a hollowed-out breakfast grapefruit will be picked clean and then become a toy.

BEWARE!

There are some human foods that are toxic to dogs, such as grapes, raisins and sultanas, and also 'human grade' chocolate. Research on the internet for a comprehensive list.

FEEDING A PUPPY

Your puppy should be eating four small meals a day when you bring him home: breakfast, lunch, tea and an early supper. He should no longer need puppy milk, but by all means give him a very occasional drink of milk if you wish – as a treat. Your dog may also enjoy a drink of warm tea with milk - but *do not* add sugar.

Water should be accessible all day - and will need to be refreshed regularly, as it will become very 'slobbery' from your Basset washing his mouth out.

If you plan to change the diet from what the breeder has been feeding, do so gradually and bear in mind that a puppy will require up to 27 per cent protein. Some puppy foods do contain higher amounts of protein, but these may cause growth problems in Bassets.

Your new puppy should have 'comfortable', formed, stools; they should not be at all runny or contain blood. Try to see your puppy relieve himself before leaving his breeder – never accept a puppy with a large worm burden or with explosive, runny,

effect. Look for the label on the packaging - if it just states that the food contains permitted antioxidants and colourants, it is best to leave it on the shelf. It is far better to purchase a product that states that the food preservative is from natural products, such as vitamin E and rosemary extract, with mixed tocopherols for the protection of oils against oxidation.

When you have decided the best feeding regime and food for your Basset Hound, the amount of extra dog biscuits and treats

given should also be taken into consideration, as the calorie content of many commercial dog treats is very high. Ideal food treats are, therefore, fresh vegetables (such as chopped carrot, parsnip, turnip, or tomato, cabbage leaves and/or leaf stalks, sprouts, cauliflower, fresh peas and beans), or fruits (such as banana, orange, pineapple, apple, and pear). A Basset will relish the skin of a freshly peeled apple or pear; a piece of fresh melon or pineapple skin, even the skin of some of the smaller sweeter

foul-smelling or bloody stools.

Any prolonged period of diarrhoea can cause an intussuscepted bowel, i.e. an enfolding of one part of the bowel back into itself, and only immediate surgery can save you pet. If your puppy normally has good stools, then suddenly goes from one extreme to the other, watch what he is eating in the garden. Bluebell leaves are one of the plants that have been known to cause this problem.

FEEDING REGIME

When your puppy first comes home, feed at approximately four hourly intervals. It is all too easy to underfeed a puppy, so slightly increase the size of the meals according to appetite. During the period of rapid growth – up to about four months old – be prepared for many of these slight increases! It is always better for the puppy to leave a little food in the dish than not have enough food. If the puppy does not come away from the dish with a bulging tummy or does not increase his intake, there may be something amiss and you may need to take advice. Remember, a baby puppy should have no waist and should be well covered.

By about five to six months, your puppy will only need three larger meals though not, necessarily, a reduced daily intake. If you are feeding a complete food, consider purchasing the junior grade, which is about 24 per cent protein level. Your puppy should be looking a little more streamlined and have a definite

waist. Now is the time to start keeping a check on your Basset's weight to ensure he does not pile on the pounds.

By about 12 months, two adult-sized meals will be required, fed morning and evening. Then, by about 15-16 months, the protein level of the complete food can be reduced to about 20 per cent, which is adult maintenance. It is very important not to feed a diet that is too high in protein; a Basset does not need it and may become hyperactive, with resultant growth plate damage or, in certain lines, a condition known as panosteitis (see Chapter Eight: Happy and Healthy).

Liquidised leftovers from *your* main meal will make small amounts of interesting gravy if your Basset Hound becomes a little picky and does not eat (but don't overdo it). This may happen in hot weather.

The older, less active dog will require a reduced protein level. Manufacturers of complete diets take this into account and produce

a 17-18 per cent protein level food with, perhaps, some joint aid added specially for the senior.

MONITORING WEIGHT

Start to keep a check on your dog's weight from six months of age. Bear in mind that an adult dog will weigh somewhere around 28 kgs (62-65 lbs), and the puppy's weight is pro rata dependent on size.

If you can clearly see each rib on your dog, the poor thing is not getting enough to eat, so you will need to feed larger quantities or extra meals. Consider if you are feeding too much protein and not enough carbohydrate.

Different dogs have different feeding requirements. To keep your dog at the correct weight, be guided by what you see and feel – not by misguided comments of non-Basset people. You should be able to feel your dog's ribs, using very slight pressure, but not be able to see them. It may be helpful to take your Basset for regular weigh-ins at your local

Do not make a sudden change in diet as this could lead to gastric upset.

veterinary practice so you spot any deviation from the norm at an early stage.

THE OVERWEIGHT ADULT BASSET

With regards to the ideal average weight for a Basset Hound (see Monitoring Weight above), bear in mind that bitches are somewhat lighter in weight than males. If you cannot feel each individual rib without pressing hard, your dog is too fat. You will need to feed smaller meals, give more exercise, and cut out treats.

If your dog is still not losing enough weight, mix about a quarter to a third (depending on the size) of white shredded cabbage, a tin of pilchards and some bran. Replace *each* daily meal with the cabbage mixture, and your dog will feel full and satisfied. You can only use the 'crash' (cabbage) diet for a maximum of four days at a time. Once you have reduced your Basset Hound's weight, you must ensure that you keep it at the right level to allow him to live a long and healthy life.

It is cruel to any dog to allow him to become overweight, though a Basset will look at this from his own perspective and consider you cruel not to allow him to eat his fill three or four times a day! Two meals a day are sufficient for an adult, and the quantity should always be tailored to how much exercise your Basset is getting. Two small meals daily

An adult will do best on two meals a day.

are better than one large meal a day; it has been suggested that a single large meal can trigger bloat (see page 141).

EXERCISING YOUR BASSET

With reference to the potential problems of growth-plate damage, exercise should be carefully monitored and limited for the first 12 to 14 months of your Basset Hound's life. However, this is not to say that you should give your Basset *no* exercise at all.

Walks should be at your hound's own pace on a soft surface, such as grass or a sandy beach, and a little free running should be permitted. Your Basset

may run after a gently thrown ball, but only for a short period. Long, steady walking on a hard surface, such as pavement or road, is not recommended – though, again, that does not mean to say that a certain amount of controlled walking should not be allowed.

Once your Basset Hound is about 14-15 months old you can take him hiking, jogging, running beside your bike, playing football – or any other rough, tough game you both enjoy.

COAT CARE

Like humans, dogs shed hair regularly – it is just more noticeable. Basset Hounds have a double coat: a strong, straight-haired topcoat, which the natural oils keep waterproof and shiny, and a soft, rather fluffy, undercoat that keeps them warm. House dogs shed their coat all the year round and need constant grooming to remove the dead hair. Hounds kept in unheated kennels grow a very thick coat over the winter months.

A regular brush with a hound glove to pull out the loose coat will keep your Basset's coat waterproof and in good order. Unless your hound has rolled in, or on, something horrible while out walking, regular bathing is not recommended, as it will soften the coat and remove the natural oils that keep it waterproof – consequently, more grooming will be necessary. On the occasions

GROWTH-PLATE DAMAGE

In order to understand the dangers of growth-plate damage, we first need to understand what is happening to the skeleton as a Basset Hound grows.

In a long bone (so named because they are the 'long' bones of the limbs, just like our arms and legs), the growth plates are situated at each end of the shaft; they are separated from the shaft by cartilage until growth is complete. With the Basset Hound, the damage usually occurs in the bones of the foreleg, at the base of the ulna, and this part of the leg can stop growing (see page 138 for further information). The inner part of the leg (the radius) will continue to grow with the result that the foot will turn outwards and, in some severe cases, the dog will not be able to stand still and balance without bringing the shoulder forward, thus causing further joint problems in older age. Similar growth-plate damage can occur in the same shortened bones, but at the growth plate close to the elbow. This is sometimes misdiagnosed as elbow dysplasia.

Growth-plate damage can happen in a badly run breeding establishment, but it is most often caused by lack of care by new owners where the puppy has been allowed to do any or all of the following:

* Exercise on hard surfaces
* Go up or down steps
* Jump out of the car (Dog ramps for cars are made commercially, though a handyman could perhaps make one quite cheaply.)
* Jump on and off furniture.

Problems may arise if a puppy is picked up by a child and is accidentally dropped – even if it is only a short distance to the ground. Care must also be taken if an adult picks up the puppy. When the pup is set on the ground, he must be lowered gently so he is in a sitting position.

A young hound should be prevented from playing rough games with bigger dogs. The growth plates in the bones of the front limbs – particularly the lower part of the ulna – can be easily damaged. The growth plates of the humerus (upper arm) continue the growth a little longer than those for the lower arm and can suffer some damage from a knock-on effect.

It can take as long as 12 to 14 months for some growth plates to mature and a Basset will not reach full maturity until he is about three years old.

Growth-plate damage has more serious effects in an achondroplastic breed than in a breed with a 'normal' limb length. Later in life, this damage can lead to arthritic problems in the whole of the forequarters as strain has been placed on the other joints.

Growth plate damage will have long lasting repercussions.

when you bath your Basset, you may consider giving a final rinse using diluted benzyle benzoate emulsion (used as a cure for scabies in humans and sweet itch in horses), which can be obtained from the vet or pharmacist. The dog should be thoroughly wet before applying the emulsion, but it can be very useful in reducing the likelihood of your dog acquiring fleas and other external parasites.

If you have been walking in woodland or field edges, examine your hound for ticks; these can be removed with a specialist tick hook (see Chapter 8).

Some Basset Hounds can suffer from sweaty areas under the chin, in the armpits and the inside of the legs. If left untreated, these can be areas where natural yeasts may flourish and form a brown, smelly, waxy coating over the skin. If your Basset Hound wears his collar at all times, do pay

special attention to his throat, around his dewlap, which may get very sweaty and sore and encourage yeast growth. If your Basset has been walking in damp conditions, do ensure these areas are properly dried. The cream used for treating athlete's foot in humans often alleviates the problem.

EARS
Because the Basset Hound's pendulous ear leather encloses the ear canal, it can become rather sweaty, smelly and waxy. Ears therefore need regular weekly checking and cleaning – just because the leather hides them, you must not forget them.

Ear cleaning preparations can be bought from your local pet store, or you can use benzyle benzoate emulsion. However, do not poke cotton-wool or a tissue deep down into the ear; if you suspect that there is a foreign

body deep inside the ear, take your Basset Hound to the vet who will be able to remove it without damage.

If your Basset is constantly scratching or shaking his head, he may have become infected with ear mites, which can be acquired from cats or even wild rabbits.

Once a dog is infected, it takes daily bathing in an insecticidal preparation before the mites are eradicated. The dog's bed and living area also needs to be cleared and cleaned daily until they are completely eradicated.

NAILS
A dog's nails – like our own – need trimming on a very regular basis to ensure correct growth and comfort. The breeder should have started this while the puppies were still in the nest and, hopefully, you will be given a lesson in nail trimming before bringing your puppy home. Once

Once your Basset is fully grown, he will enjoy as much exercise as you can give him.

ROUTINE CARE

Regular brushing keeps the coat in good order and aids circulation.

The ears should be checked and cleaned on a regular basis.

It may help if you recruit an assistant to help with nail cutting.

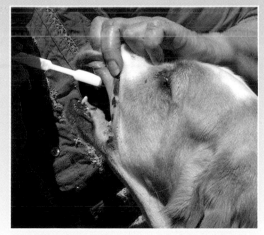

Accustom your Basset to teeth cleaning from an early age.

a Basset Hound is old enough for long walks, the nails will keep fairly short – but not all at the same level – so unless your hound has a perfect foot, some trimming will be necessary. Consider how uncomfortable you would be if you had to walk everywhere with very long toenails!

Nails can be trimmed using either a Dremel, which is a small electric sanding tool used by wood craftsmen, or by using special clippers for canine nails. A special guillotine nail-clipper is recommended, this will shave the nail rather than squashing it, as many of the scissor type of clippers do.

If you cut into the quick – the centre, fleshy part of the nail – it will bleed profusely for a short while, which will probably be more upsetting for you than it is for the dog. Using guillotine clippers, you are able to shave small sections off around the quick, leaving it a little proud so it will not bleed.

Nail trimming is better done as a two-man job – you can sit on the floor with the Basset between your legs, lying on his back against your chest, and the other person can easily reach each foot. When you have finished, remember to reward your Basset with a treat. After a few sessions, provided that you have shaved around the quick instead of cutting straight across – your Basset will see the clippers and position himself for nail cutting, knowing that he will earn a treat.

If you have purchased your puppy from a breeder who has not given any foot care to the puppies, it is worth paying a dog groomer to give you a lesson. Nail trimming must be continued for the rest of your Basset Hound's life so it will be of enormous benefit if your Basset accepts the procedure without too much fuss. An old Basset with overgrown toenails will walk on the wrong part of his foot, putting extra strain on any arthritic joints.

If your Basset has dewclaws on the inside of his front legs, do not forget to clip them, otherwise they may curl round as they grow and catch the skin.

TEETH

Do not be too vigorous in cleaning teeth with a young puppy who is teething and has a very sore mouth. However, once the teeth are through, they will need to be cleaned on a routine basis. As with nail clipping, initially it is easier as a two-man job.

CAR TRAVEL

It is not safe to allow your Basset Hound to travel loose in the car;

THE SHOW DOG

The care for a show dog should be little different to that for your companion Basset Hound. He needs to be healthy, his teeth clean, his ears clean, his nails short and his coat needs to be well brushed to ensure that there is no loose undercoat. His topcoat needs to shine with health. If he is to be bathed, it is best to do this a couple of days before the show so that the coat has time to settle – bathing removes the natural waterproofing oils and softens the coat. Because the function of the breed is that of a hunting hound – even though a show dog has never hunted in his life – it is essential that the coat is waterproof, and it is the natural oils and strong topcoat that keep it so.

The hardest part of exhibiting a Basset Hound is keeping his nose off the ground when you are gaiting him!

CAR TRAVEL

A Basset should never be allowed to jump in or out of a car.
Teach him from a puppy to wait for your help.

if you have to brake suddenly he may injure himself or those travelling in the car. Seat belts for dogs are available at specialist stores; they are made in different sizes and have a padded area at the front and a special 'twizzle' fastener to the car point, which enables the dog to turn round and round before lying down without becoming stuck.

It is recommended that such a seat harness is used, with a hammock fitted round the back seat head-rest and the head-rest opposite on the front seat. The hammock doubles the space for the dog to lie and will prevent him slipping forward into the footwell in case of emergency braking.

In most cases, the crate you have purchased for your dog's bed in the house will be too large to fit in the car. Purpose-made crates are available for most makes of estate car; the only problem is that they are not always interchangeable if you change the make of car. A well-fitted dog guard against the back seat, and a fitted frame with a door against the back door of the car, will enclose the boot area safely. You may wish to further ensure your dog's safety by the use of a car harness.

A Basset Hound is not a breed that can easily – or safely – jump in or out of a car, and he is too heavy to lift. The best solution is to buy a ramp, and then you can be confident that your Basset will not damage himself as he gets in and out of the car.

HOT DOGS

Never leave your dog in a parked car. On sunny days a parked car can soon become very hot, even when parked in the shade. Also remember that the sun does move, and what was a shady spot at the time of parking may be in full sunlight an hour later. On cloudy summer days, it can soon become hot in a parked car, and winter sun can also cause the temperature to rise in a parked vehicle.

When travelling on hot days, it is important to allow cool air to circulate for your dog. If your vehicle does not have shaded windows, consider fitting blinds to the rear area.

Dogs do become thirsty while travelling, so take plenty of water and a bowl and make frequent stops. Special dishes can be obtained, which contain the water without spilling during travelling – though a Basset may see this as an extra toy, which somewhat defeats the object!

A Basset can easily overheat in warm weather so make sure you take a supply of drinking water on days out.

If you do not have a ramp, you will need to train your Basset in the following way:

- Encourage your dog to place his front feet just inside the car.
- You lift his hind legs (just below the hock) and let him walk in - just like a wheelbarrow.
- To get your Basset out of the car, let him sit across your knee and let his hindquarters reach the ground first, then lower the front legs carefully to the ground.

Never let a puppy jump out of a car – you are liable to damage his growth plates. Adults can also suffer injury to the wrist, elbow or shoulder joints.

TRAVEL SICKNESS
Some Basset Hounds may suffer from travel sickness. This can be eased by providing a well-padded mattress type of bed, and ensuring that windows are covered so that your dog cannot see out. If he is travelling in a crate, a damp towel hung over the sides will alleviate the sickness. Be matter of fact with the dog about the condition rather than sympathetic and, as he grows older, he will probably find it easier to cope.

NEUTERING
Very early neutering can alter the growth pattern of both dogs and bitches and can result in a permanently immature hound. The sex hormones play a part in the completion of bone growth. Neutering delays the closure of the growth plates in the bones and, since the growth plates in different bones close at different times, this may result in a Basset with slightly unnatural proportions. This could have a long-term impact on the performance and durability of the joints, i.e. a cause of arthritis.

Some veterinary research shows that a number of long-time health problems, resulting from early neutering may exceed any associated health benefits, although this may vary from dog to dog. Early neutering may reduce the risk of mammary cancer and testicular cancer, but can increase the risk of urinary incontinence in both dogs and bitches. Neutering, if done before maturity, could increase the risk of osteosarcoma (bone cancer).

Most responsible breeders consider that it is better to neuter a bitch after her first season and a dog after a year old. However, neutering (at any age) also increases the risk of obesity in both dogs and bitches – but this can be managed by giving increased exercise and a reduced diet.

CARING FOR THE OLDER DOG
As we grow older and a little slower, so do our dogs – though because their life span is not as long as ours, it is more obvious in our pets. The older dog will sleep more and probably go into a far deeper sleep than when he was younger – and a very senior dog may even have to be woken when it is time for his walk! It is most important to continue the exercise to keep the joints supple and the brain active. The sights and smells along the route will keep your Basset Hound's mind as alert as much as reading the newspaper or watching the television news does for us. It is just a little thing – but better than allowing your hound to sleep his life away.

Two or three short walks are more beneficial than one long expedition, which may be too strenuous. You may find that you have to initiate play by throwing a ball for your hound to fetch, although throwing a favourite food treat, such as a piece of fruit or vegetable, sometimes works better with a Basset Hound!

If you are feeding a complete food, you can change to the senior variety with a lower protein level and joint aid additives. If you feed a mixture of meat and biscuit, mix more vegetables and less meat to the meal.

An old Basset may have problems with his teeth without you realising. Even if you have followed a regular regime of tooth care since puppyhood, you may not recognise that there is a problem, so regular veterinary check-ups are recommended.

If you have another dog and he is constantly licking at the old dog's mouth, seek advice from your vet. This happened some years ago with our 10-year-old bitch. An X-ray showed that quite a number of teeth would have to be removed from both the upper and lower jaws, with a possibility that this would loosen the remaining teeth. The decision was taken to remove all her teeth.

The bitch recovered very quickly and very well, and was soon playing with the other dogs. She had no trouble in eating – to the extent that any spillage of hard biscuit was soon hoovered up – she could get more into her mouth at a time than the other dogs – and she would go into a crate in order that no one else could steal her gains. Though, to her dismay, human intervention did ensure that she did not eat it all! She lived for another four and a half years and enjoyed her food throughout that time.

LETTING GO

The last kindness you can give your Basset is to let him go if he is very ill or uncomfortable. An old dog sleeps a lot but he should still have a keen interest in life and what goes on around him. It is your duty to ensure your old friend enjoys a good quality of life.

Some vets will visit the home to give a lethal injection; others will prefer you to visit the surgery. If you do go to the veterinary surgery, you will need another person (not closely involved with the dog) to be your driver and bring you home safely.

Coping with the loss of a canine family member is exactly the same as coping with the loss of a human family member – they are both very much a part of your life and the grieving is the same. It is something that is very private and different for

An elderly Basset will want to take life at his own pace.

In time you will be able to look back and remember all the happy times you spent with your beloved Basset.

everybody. If you have another dog, or a cat who was a close friend, they too will be mourning, though animals seem to accept death better than we humans.

Do not rush out and immediately purchase another dog – even if it is of another breed. The new dog will sense your sadness and wonder what he is doing wrong – and he will do everything wrong just because he is not your own Basset and so does not know the ropes – the expected behaviour. Inevitably, you will make comparisons.

Give yourself time to mourn in private, but do consider that if you already have another dog, he will be just as sad at the loss of his companion – though he will probably be more worried about you.

When you decide the time is right to bring another Basset into the house, try to consider dispassionately if you are looking for a clone of your previous Basset. Will you expect your new companion to understand and do everything the same as your old companion? If this is the case, you are not yet ready to share your home with another dog.

If you can accept that this new companion is going to be his own person, then you are ready to go and find him.

SOCIALISATION AND TRAINING

Chapter 6

When you decided to bring a Basset Hound into your life, you probably had dreams of how it was going to be: long walks together, cosy evenings with a Basset lying devotedly at your feet, and, whenever you returned home, there would always be a special welcome waiting for you.

There is no doubt that you can achieve all this – and much more – with a Basset Hound, but like anything that is worth having, you must be prepared to put in the work. A Basset, regardless of whether he is a puppy or an adult, does not come ready trained, understanding exactly what you want and fitting perfectly into your lifestyle. A Basset has to learn his place in your family and he must discover what is acceptable behaviour.

We have a great starting point in that the breed is loving and affectionate and wants nothing more than to be with his human family. But we must also bear in mind that this is a hunting dog with an incredible sense of smell, and following a scent trail will always be his top priority. There is another important consideration: the Basset is a thinking dog, and although his intelligence cannot be disputed, he will work out what is in his best interests before deciding whether to co-operate.

THE FAMILY PACK

Dogs have been domesticated for some 14,000 years, but luckily for us, they have inherited and retained behaviour from their distant ancestor – the wolf. A Basset Hound may never have lived in the wild, but he is born with the survival skills and the mentality of a meat-eating predator who hunts in a pack. A wolf living in a pack owes its existence to mutual co-operation and an acceptance of a hierarchy, as this ensures both food and protection. A domesticated dog living in a family pack has exactly the same outlook. He wants food, companionship, and leadership – and it is your job to provide for these needs. The Basset Hound – like all the hound breeds – is slightly different, as hounds have worked on their own from time immemorial, with man following at their instigation. Even working as a pack, each Basset hunts the line individually, which is why they are also such good dogs for finding and flushing game to the gun.

YOUR ROLE

Theories about dog behaviour and methods of training go in and out of fashion, but in reality, nothing has changed from the day when wolves ventured in from the wild to join the family circle. The wolf (and equally the dog) accepts a subservient place in the family pack in return for food and protection. In a dog's eyes, you are his leader and he relies on you to make all the important decisions. This does not mean that you have to act like a dictator or a bully. You are accepted as a leader, without argument, as long as you have the right credentials. An indecisive and inconsistent owner does not, in your dog's eyes, have the right credentials to be the pack leader and your Basset may think he can bully you and take over the role. He may be slow to obey your commands, but as long as you make him obey – and never allow him to have the last word

HOW TO BE A GOOD LEADER

There are a number of guidelines to follow to establish yourself in the role of leader in a way that your Basset Hound understands and respects. If you have a puppy, you may think you don't have to take this on board for a few months, but that would be a big mistake. With a Basset it is absolutely essential to start as you mean to go on. The behaviour he learns as a puppy will continue throughout his adult life, which means that undesirable behaviour can be very difficult to rectify.

When your Basset Hound first arrives in his new home, follow these guidelines:

- Keep it simple: Decide on the rules you want your Basset to obey and always make it 100 per cent clear what is acceptable, and what is unacceptable, behaviour. Make sure the whole family – even the youngest child – knows and understands these rules.
- Be consistent: If you are not consistent about enforcing rules, how can you expect your Basset to take you seriously? There is nothing worse than allowing your Basset to sleep on the sofa one moment and then scolding him the next time he does it because he is muddy. As far as the Basset is concerned, he may as well try it on because he cannot predict your reaction. Bear in mind: inconsistency leads to insecurity.
- Get your timing right: If you are rewarding your Basset and equally if you are reprimanding him, you must respond within one to two seconds otherwise the dog will not link his behaviour with your reaction (see page 84 'How Dogs Learn').
- Read your dog's body language: Find out how to read body language and facial expressions (see page 83) so that you understand your Basset's feelings and intentions.
- Be aware of your own body language: You can also help your dog to learn by using your body language to communicate with him. For example, if you want your dog to come to you, open your arms out and look inviting. If you want your dog to stay, use a hand signal (palm flat, facing the dog) so you are effectively 'blocking' his advance.
- Tone of voice: Dogs do not speak English; they learn by associating a word with the required action. However, they are very receptive to tone of voice, so you can use your voice to praise him or to correct undesirable behaviour. If you are pleased with your Basset, praise him to the skies in a warm, happy voice. If you want to stop him raiding the bin, use a deep, stern voice when you say "No". In this situation, a Basset is quite

– he will accept his position in your pack.

The first part of the job is easy. You are the provider and you are therefore respected because you supply food. In a Basset's eyes, you must be the ultimate hunter, because a day never goes by when you cannot find food. The second part of the leader's job description is straightforward, but for some reason we find it hard to achieve. In order for a dog to accept his place in the family pack, he must respect his leader as the decision-maker. A low-ranking pack animal does not question authority; he is perfectly happy to see someone else shoulder the responsibility. Problems will only arise if you cut a poor figure as leader and the dog feels he should mount a challenge for the top-ranking role.

likely to 'freeze', and if there is no further command, he will continue the 'raid'. You will need to make him come right away from the bin – and then make the bin inaccessible.

- Give one command only: If you keep repeating a command, or keeping changing it, your Basset will think you are babbling and will probably ignore you. If your Basset does not respond the first time you ask, make it simple by using a treat to lure him into position and then you can reward him for a correct response.
- Daily reminders: A Basset Hound has a tendency to follow his own agenda, and may forget his manners from time to time. Rather than coming down on him like a ton of bricks when he does something wrong, try to prevent bad manners by daily reminders of good manners. For example:
  i Do not let your dog barge ahead of you when you are going through a door.
  ii Never let him leap out of the car the moment you open the door (which could be potentially lethal, as well as being disrespectful).
  iii Do not let him eat from your hand when you are at the table.
  iv Do not let him 'win' a toy at the end of a play session and then make off with it. You 'own' his toys and you 'allow' him to play with them. Your Basset must learn to give up a toy when you ask.

Do you have what it takes to be a firm, fair and consistent leader?

READING THE SIGNS

If you watch two dogs meet and greet, you will learn a lot about canine body language.

Both dogs are on lead, which slightly inhibits their behaviour, but they are both giving off positive, friendly signals.

They move in nose to nose, neither dog feels threatened.

The dog on the left is keen to start a game....

That's a bit full on for the dog on the right.

UNDERSTANDING YOUR BASSET HOUND

Body language is an important means of communication between dogs, which they use to make friends, to assert status and to avoid conflict. It is important to get on your dog's wavelength by understanding his body language and reading his facial expressions. Those who are new to the breed may think that Bassets all share a similar doleful expression, but those who know Bassets become very good at reading their individual expressions, which may change with a tilt of the head, a lift of the ears, or a furrowed brow.

- A positive body posture and a wagging tail indicate a happy, confident dog. A relaxed and happy Basset has a slight 'lift' to the top of the ear, and the front of the ear will curl slightly inwards towards the cheek; their eyes have a different sparkle, and their mouths are often slightly open when they are laughing!
- A crouched body posture, with ears dropped and fitting closer to the head (sometimes flattened instead of the graceful inward curl), and tail down show that a dog is being submissive. A dog may do this when he is being told off or if a more assertive dog approaches him.
- A bold dog will stand tall, looking strong and alert. His ears will be lifted at the top and the ear leather will be curled strongly inwards; his tail will be held high.
- A dog who raises his hackles (lifting the fur along his topline)

is trying to look as scary as possible.
- A playful dog will go down on his front legs while standing on his hind legs in a bow position. This friendly invitation says, "I'm no threat, let's play."
- A dominant, aggressive dog will meet other dogs with a hard stare. If he is challenged, he may bare his teeth and growl and the corners of his mouth will be drawn forward. You will know a Basset is on the offensive if you see well-lifted ears (the leather almost folded flat in half), and the tail carried rigidly sabre-like. He may give a very stiff wag of the end two or three vertebrae. Sometimes he will shiver. If you meet another dog to whom your Basset exhibits this behaviour, stand still with a very firm grip on the lead and ask the owner of the other dog to walk round you at a good distance. A 28- to 30-kilo Basset is very heavy if he lunges forwards.
- A nervous dog will often show aggressive behaviour as a means of self-protection. If threatened, this dog will lower his head and flatten his ears. The corners of his mouth may be drawn back and he may bark or whine. Ear carriage is the same as a submissive dog; tail carriage is the same as the aggressive dog.
- The Basset Hound is a notorious thief, so if you spot your Basset walking with jaunty air – his ears lifted and folded slightly inwards – as he makes his way towards a corner or at the back of his crate with his neck arched and his head down, you can bet his has

a 'secret' (a stolen toy or some food he has scavenged), which he is trying to hide from you.
- Be aware of the Basset 'look'. A Basset will wait at the door, staring at it or looking at you, waiting for the door to miraculously open so he can go out to relieve himself. He knows what he wants, and thinks that you should be on his wavelength. He is not looking at you devotedly – he is asking to go out. Ignore the Basset 'look' at your peril.

GIVING REWARDS

Why should your Basset Hound do as you ask? If you follow the guidelines given above, your Basset should respect your authority, but what about the time when he has found a really enticing scent? The answer is that you must always be the most interesting, the most attractive and the most irresistible person in your Basset's eyes. It would be nice to think that you could achieve this by personality alone, but most of us need a little extra help. You need to find out what is the biggest reward for your dog. A Basset Hound loves his food, so he will be quite happy to be 'bribed' into doing what you want. The logic of doing something *you* ask to get something *he* wants appeals to the Basset mind. Decide on a reward word – a long drawn out "Yeahhh" or "Goood" given at the same time as the treat becomes just as important as the treat itself, and can be used to reward unexpected 'good' behaviour when a treat is not instantly to hand.

Most Bassets consider a food treat to be worth working for.

A game with a favourite toy is preferred by some dogs.

Bassets are very playful dogs and many will be motivated to 'work' for a toy. However, a Basset is very indiscriminate when it comes to selecting toys – and sees everything from a book to an electric cable as a potential plaything. You will need to be very strict and keep a toy solely for training purposes so that it accrues special value.

When you are teaching a dog a new exercise, you should reward your Basset frequently. When he knows the exercise or command, reward him randomly so that he keeps on responding to you in a positive manner.

If your Basset Hound does something extra special, like responding (fairly instantly) to a recall in the park, make sure he really knows how pleased you are by giving him a handful of treats or having an extra-long play with his toy. If he gets a bonanza reward, he is more likely to come back on future occasions because you have proved to be even more rewarding than his previous activity.

TOP TREATS
Some trainers grade treats depending on what they are asking the dog to do. A dog may get a low-grade treat (such as a piece of dry food) to reward good behaviour on a random basis, such as sitting when you open a door or allowing you to examine his teeth. High-grade treats (which may be cooked liver, sausage or cheese, or small cubes of dried fish skin) may be reserved for training new

exercises or for use in the park when you want a really good recall, for example.

Whatever type of treat you use, remember to subtract it from your Basset's daily food ration. Fat dogs are lethargic, prone to health problems and will almost certainly have a shorter life expectancy, so reward your Basset, but always keep a check on his figure!

HOW DO DOGS LEARN?
It is not difficult to get inside your Basset Hound's head and understand how he learns, as it is not dissimilar to the way we learn. Dogs learn by conditioning: they find out that specific behaviours produce specific consequences. This is known as operant conditioning or consequence

THE CLICKER REVOLUTION

Karen Pryor pioneered the technique of clicker training when she was working with dolphins. It is very much a continuation of Pavlov's work and makes full use of association learning. Karen wanted to mark 'correct' behaviour at the precise moment it happened. She found it was impossible to toss a fish to a dolphin when it was in mid-air, when she wanted to reward it. Her aim was to establish a conditioned response so the dolphin knew that it had performed correctly and a reward would follow.

The solution was the clicker: a small matchbox-shaped training aid, with a metal tongue that makes a click when it is pressed. To begin with, the dolphin had to learn that a click meant that food was coming. The dolphin then learnt that it must 'earn' a click in order to get a reward. Clicker training has been used with many different animals, most particularly with dogs, and it has proved hugely successful. It is a great aid for pet owners and is also widely used by professional trainers who are training highly specialised skills.

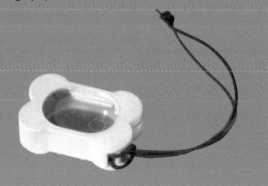

learning. Consequences have to be immediate or clearly linked to the behaviour, as a dog sees the world in terms of action and result. Dogs will quickly learn if an action has a bad consequence or a good consequence.

Dogs also learn by association. This is known as classical conditioning or association learning. It is the type of learning made famous by Pavlov's experiment with dogs. Pavlov presented dogs with food and measured their salivary response (how much they drooled). Then he rang a bell just before presenting the food. At first, the dogs did not salivate until the food was presented. But after a while they learnt that the sound of the bell meant that food was coming and so they salivated when they heard the bell. A dog needs to learn the association in order for it to have any meaning. For example, a dog that has never seen a lead before will be completely indifferent to it. A dog that has learnt that a lead means he is going for a walk will get excited the second he sees the lead; he has learnt to associate a lead with a walk.

BE POSITIVE

The most effective method of training dogs is to use their ability to learn by consequence and to teach that the behaviour you want produces a good consequence. For example, if you ask your Basset Hound to "Sit" and reward him with a treat, he will learn that it is worth his while to sit on command because it will lead to a treat. He is far more likely to repeat the behaviour, and the behaviour will become stronger, because it results in a positive outcome. This method of training is known as positive reinforcement and it generally leads to a happy, co-operative dog that is willing to work and a handler who has fun training their dog.

The opposite approach is negative reinforcement. This is far less effective and often results in a poor relationship between dog and owner. In this method of training, you ask your Basset Hound to "Sit" and if he does not respond, you deliver a sharp yank on the training collar or push his rear to the ground. The dog learns that not responding to your command has a bad consequence and he may be less likely to ignore you in the future. However, it may well

have a bad consequence for you, too. A dog that is treated in this way may associate harsh handling with the handler and become aggressive or fearful. Instead of establishing a pattern of willing co-operation, you are establishing a relationship built on coercion.

GETTING STARTED

When you train your Basset Hound you will develop your own techniques as you get to know what motivates him. You may decide to get involved with clicker training or you may prefer to go for a simple command-and-reward formula. Some Basset owners prefer this, as they think clicker training has a tendency to suppress the breed's natural fun-loving exuberance. This is a matter of personal choice and seeing what works best with your Basset. However, it does not really matter

what form of training you use, as long as it is based on positive, reward-based methods.

There are a few important guidelines to bear in mind when you are training your Basset:

- Find a training area that is free from distractions, particularly when you are just starting out. A Basset Hound cannot resist interesting scents, so it may be easier to train him indoors to begin with.
- Keep training sessions short, especially with young puppies that have very short attention spans.
- Do not train if you are in a bad mood or if you are on a tight schedule – the training session will be doomed to failure.
- If you are using a toy as a reward, make sure it is only available when you are training.
- If you are using food treats, make sure they are bite-size and easy to swallow; you don't want to hang about while your Basset chews on his treat.
- Do not attempt to train your Basset after he has eaten, or soon after returning from exercise. He will either be too full up to care about food treats or too tired to concentrate.
- When you are training, move around your allocated area so that your dog does not think that an exercise can only be performed in one place.
- If your Basset is finding an exercise difficult, try not to get frustrated. Go back a step and praise him for his effort. You will probably find he is more successful when you try again at

You may find it hard to get your Basset's attention if you are training outside where he can pick up interesting scents.

the next training session.
- If a training session is not going well – either because you are in the wrong frame of mind or the dog is not focusing – ask your Basset to do something you know he can do (such as a trick he enjoys performing) and then you can reward him with a food treat or a play with his favourite toy, ending the session on a happy, positive note.
- Do not train for too long. You need to end a training session on a high, with your Basset wanting more, rather than making him sour by asking too much from him.

In the exercises that follow, clicker training is introduced and followed, but all the exercises will work without the use of a clicker.

INTRODUCING A CLICKER

This is very easy, and the intelligent Basset Hound will learn about the clicker in record time – although you may need to vary the treats and be creative in your training to he maintains his enthusiasm. Clicker training can be combined with attention training, which is a very useful tool and can be used on many different occasions.
- Prepare some treats and go to an area that is totally free from distractions. Allow your Basset to wander and, when he stops to look at you, click and reward by throwing him a treat. This means he will not crowd you, but will go looking for the treat. Repeat a couple of times. If your Basset is very easily distracted, you may need to start this exercise with the dog on a lead.
- After a few clicks, your Basset will understand that if he hears a click, he will get a treat. He must now learn that he must 'earn' a click. This time, when your Basset looks at you, wait a little longer before clicking and then reward him. If your Basset is on a lead but responding well, try him off the lead.
- When your Basset is working for a click and giving you his attention, you can introduce a cue or command word, such as "Watch". Repeat a few times, using the cue. You now have a Basset Hound that understands the clicker and will give you his attention when you ask him to "Watch".

TRAINING EXERCISES

The Basset Hound has a reputation for being stubborn, particularly if he does not see there is anything to gain. Make sure you keep training sessions light-hearted, and break them up with treats and play sessions. Capitalise on your Basset's sense of humour, and play games with him so that he enjoys interacting with you.

If your Basset is not co-operating, do not become confrontational – and never make the mistake of attempting to manhandle your Basset into position   it will not work! If you are struggling with an exercise and your Basset appears to have gone on strike, be creative and try to think of a new way of teaching that will appeal to the Basset mind. Remember, a Basset is a highly intelligent dog and, as far as he is concerned, there should be a good reason for everything he does.

THE SIT

This is the easiest exercise to teach, so it is rewarding for both you and your Basset Hound.
- Choose a tasty treat and hold it just above your puppy's nose. As

With practice, your Basset will respond to a verbal cue and you will not need to lure him into position.

You may need to encourage your Basset to stay in the Down by applying gentle pressure on his shoulders.

Give lots of praise when you are training the Recall.

he looks up at the treat, he will naturally go into the 'Sit'. As soon as he is in position, reward him.

- Repeat the exercise and when your pup understands what you want, introduce the "Sit" command.
- You can practise the Sit exercise at mealtimes by holding out the bowl and waiting for your dog to sit. Most Bassets learn this one very quickly!

THE DOWN
Work hard at this exercise because a reliable 'Down' is useful in many different situations, and an instant 'Down' can be a lifesaver.

- You can start with your dog in a 'Sit', or it is just as effective to teach it when the dog is standing. Hold a treat just below your puppy's nose and slowly lower it towards the ground. The treat acts as a lure and your puppy will follow it, first going down on his forequarters and then bringing his hindquarters down as he tries to get the treat.
- Make sure you close your fist

around the treat and only reward your puppy with the treat when he is in the correct position. If your puppy is reluctant to go 'Down', you can apply gentle pressure on his shoulders to encourage him to go into the correct position.
- When your puppy is following the treat and going into position, introduce a verbal command.
- Build up this exercise over a period of time, each time waiting a little longer before giving the reward, so the puppy learns to stay in the 'Down' position.

SECRET WEAPON

You can build up a strong recall by using another form of association learning. Buy a whistle and when you are giving your Basset Hound his food, peep on the whistle. You can choose the type of signal you want to give: two short peeps or one long whistle, for example. Within a matter of days, your dog will learn that the sound of the whistle means that food is coming.

Now transfer the lesson outside. Arm yourself with some tasty treats and the whistle. Allow your Basset to run free in the garden and, after a couple of minutes, use the whistle. The dog has already learnt to associate the whistle with food, so he will come towards you. Immediately reward him with a treat and lots of

praise. Repeat the lesson a few times in the garden, so you are confident that your dog is responding before trying it in the park. Make sure you always have some treats in your pocket when you go for a walk and your dog will quickly learn how rewarding it is to come to you.

THE RECALL

It is never too soon to begin training your Basset Hound the recall. The *raison d'être* of the breed is to hunt, and so there is never anything more important than following a scent trail. All Basset owners must fully understand this, and then work to get the best results. You may never get a Basset with a lightning fast recall, but, ideally, you want a dog that you can exercise off the lead, as long as you are in a safe environment.

Hopefully, the breeder will have already started recall training by calling the puppies in from outside and rewarding them with some treats scattered on the floor. But even if this has not been the case, you will find that a puppy arriving in his new home is highly responsive. His chief desire is to follow you and to be with you. Capitalise on this from day one by getting your pup's attention and calling him to you in a bright, excited tone of voice.

- Practise in the garden. When your puppy is busy exploring, get his attention by clapping

and calling his name. As he runs towards you, introduce the verbal command "Come", making sure you sound happy and exciting, so your puppy wants to come to you. When he responds, give him lots of praise.
- If your puppy is slow to respond, try running away a few paces or jumping up and down. It doesn't matter how silly you look, the key issue is to get your puppy's attention and then make yourself irresistible!
- In a dog's mind, coming when

called should be regarded as the best fun because he knows he is always going to be rewarded. Never make the mistake of telling your dog off, no matter how slow he is to respond, as you will undo all your previous hard work.

• When you call your Basset to you, make sure he comes up close enough to be touched. He must understand that "Come" means that he should come right up to you, otherwise he will think that he can approach and then veer off when it suits him.

• When you are free running your dog, make sure you have his favourite toy or a pocket full of treats so you can reward him at intervals throughout the walk when you call him to you. Do not allow your dog to free run and only call him back at the

end of the walk to clip on his lead. An intelligent Basset Hound will soon realise that the recall means the end of his walk and then end of fun – so who can blame him for not wanting to come back?

TRAINING LINE

This is the equivalent of a very long lead, which you can buy at a pet store, or you can make your own with a length of rope. The training line is attached to your Basset Hound's collar and should be around 15 feet (4.5 metres) in length.

The purpose of the training line is to prevent your Basset from disobeying you so that he never has the chance to get into bad habits. For example, when you call your Basset and he ignores you, you can immediately pick up the end of the training line and

call him again. By picking up the line you will have attracted his attention and if you call in an excited, happy voice, your Basset will come to you. The moment he reaches you, give him a tasty treat so he is instantly rewarded for making the 'right' decision.

Many Basset owners use a training line if they are involved in an occupation, such as fishing, which involves some inattention on the part of the owner. You can purchase a tie-out stake that screws into the ground and your Basset can be attached to this, on his training line – or on a long lead – so he has the freedom to move and to sniff, but cannot wander off.

WALKING ON A LOOSE LEAD

This is a simple exercise, but it can be a problem with Basset Hounds who are very strong and determined if they find a scent. In most cases, owners make the mistake of wanting to get on with the expedition rather than training the dog how to walk on a lead.

In this exercise, as with all lessons that you teach your Basset Hound, you must adopt a calm, determined, no-nonsense attitude so he knows that you mean business. A Basset may not be the most obedient dog, but he should be respectful and understand that he cannot pull with all his might on the lead when he finds something worthy of his interest.

• In the early stages of lead training, allow your puppy to pick his route and follow him. He will get used to the feeling

A puppy may put up a show of resistance when you start lead training. Gentle persuasion and a food treat will usually do the trick…

of being 'attached' to you and has no reason to put up any resistance.

- Next, find a toy or a tasty treat and show it to your puppy. Let him follow the treat/toy for a few paces and then reward him.
- Build up the amount of time your pup will walk with you and when he is walking nicely by your side, introduce the verbal command "Heel" or "Close". Give lots of praise when your pup is in the correct position.
- When your pup is walking alongside you, keep focusing his attention on you by using his name and then rewarding him when he looks at you. If it is going well, introduce some changes of direction.
- Do not attempt to take your puppy out on the lead until you have mastered the basics at home. You need to be confident that your puppy accepts the lead and will focus his attention on you, when requested, before you face the challenge of a busy environment.
- If your Basset picks up a scent and tries to surge ahead, do not give in to him or he will see this as a licence to tow you round the park. You need to stop and call your dog so you have his full attention. Reward him, and do not set off again until he is in the correct position. It may take time, but your Basset Hound will eventually realise that it is more productive to walk by your side than to pull ahead.

STAYS

This is not the most exciting exercise, but it is very useful. There are many occasions when you want your Basset to stay in position, even if it is only for a few seconds. The classic example is when you want your Basset to stay in the back of the car until you have clipped on his lead. This is an important safety procedure with all dogs, but with a Basset it is even more important that he does not jump out of the car and risk injury.

When teaching this exercise, some trainers use the verbal command "Stay" when the dog is to stay in position for an extended period of time and "Wait" if the dog is to stay in position for a few seconds until you give the next command. Others trainers use a universal "Stay" to cover all situations. It all comes down to personal preference, and as long as you are consistent, your dog will understand the command he is given.

- Put your puppy in a 'Sit' or a 'Down' and use a hand signal (flat palm, facing the dog) to show he is to stay in position. Step a pace away from the dog. Wait a second, step back and reward him. If you have a lively pup, you may find it easier to train this exercise on the lead.
- Repeat the exercise, gradually increasing the distance you can leave your dog. When you return to your dog's side, praise him quietly and release him with a command, such as "OK".
- Remember to keep your body language very still when you are training this exercise and avoid eye contact with your dog. Work on this exercise over a period of time and you will build up a really reliable 'Stay'.

Build up the Stay exercise in easy stages.

SOCIALISATION

While your Basset Hound is mastering basic obedience exercises, there is other, equally important work to do with him. A Basset is not only becoming a part of your home and family, he is becoming a member of the community. He needs to be able to live in the outside world, coping calmly with every new situation that comes his way. It is your job to introduce him to as many different experiences as possible and to encourage him to behave in an appropriate manner.

In order to socialise your Basset Hound effectively, it is helpful to understand how his brain is developing and then you will get a perspective on how he sees the world.

CANINE SOCIALISATION
(Birth to 7 weeks)
This is the time when a dog learns how to be a dog. By interacting with his mother and his littermates, a young pup learns about leadership and submission. He learns to read body posture so that he understands the intentions of his mother and his siblings. A puppy that is taken away from his litter too early may always have behavioural problems with other dogs, either being fearful or aggressive.

SOCIALISATION PERIOD
7 to 12 weeks)
This is the time to get cracking and introduce your Basset puppy to as many different experiences as possible. This includes meeting different people, other dogs and animals, seeing new sights and hearing a range of sounds, from the vacuum cleaner to the roar of traffic. A puppy learns very quickly and what he learns will stay with him for the rest of his life. This is the best time for a puppy to move to a new home, as he is adaptable and ready to form deep bonds.

FEAR-IMPRINT PERIOD
(8 to 11 weeks)
This occurs during the socialisation period and it can be the cause of problems if it is not handled carefully. If a pup is exposed to a frightening or painful experience, it will lead to lasting impressions. Obviously, you will attempt to avoid frightening situations, such as your pup being bullied by a mean-spirited older dog, or a firework going off, but you cannot always protect your puppy from the unexpected. If your pup has a nasty experience, the best plan is to make light of it and distract him by offering him a treat or a game. The pup will take the lead from you and will be

A well-socialised Basset will be calm and confident in all situations.

IDEAS FOR SOCIALISATION

When you are socialising your Basset Hound, you want him to experience as many different situations as possible. Try out some of the following ideas, which will ensure your Basset has an all-round education.

If you are taking on a rescued dog and have little knowledge of his background, it is important to work through a programme of socialisation. A young puppy soaks up new experiences like a sponge, but an older dog can still learn. If a rescued dog shows fear or apprehension, treat him in exactly the same way as you would treat a youngster who is going through the second fear-imprint period (see page 94).

- Accustom your puppy to household noises, such as the vacuum cleaner, the television and the washing machine.

- Ask visitors to come to the door, wearing different types of clothing – for example, wearing a hat, a long raincoat, or carrying a stick or an umbrella.

- If you do not have children at home, make sure your Basset has a chance to meet and play with them. Go to a local park and watch children in the play area. You will not be able to take your Basset Hound inside the play area, but he will see children playing and will get used to their shouts of excitement.

- Attend puppy classes. These are designed for puppies between the ages of 12 to 20 weeks and give puppies a chance to play and interact together in a controlled,

supervised environment. Your vet will have details of a local class.

- Take a walk around some quiet streets, such as a residential area, so your Basset can get used to the sound of traffic. As he becomes more confident, progress to busier areas. Remember, your lead is like a live wire and your feelings will travel directly to your Basset. Assume a calm, confident manner and your puppy will take the lead from you and have no reason to be fearful.

- Go to a railway station. You don't have to get on a train if you don't need to, but your Basset will have the chance to experience trains, people wheeling luggage, loudspeaker announcements and going up and down stairs and over railway bridges.

- If you live in the town, plan a trip to the country. You can enjoy a day out and provide an opportunity for your Basset to see livestock, such as sheep, cattle and horses.

- One of the best places for socialising a dog is at a country fair. There will be crowds of people, livestock in pens, tractors, bouncy castles, fairground rides and food stalls.

- When your dog is over 20 weeks of age, locate a training class for adult dogs. You may find that your local training class has both puppy and adult classes.

- Join a breed club and attend a fun day or a Basset walk – both you and your dog will enjoy a great day out meeting Bassets and Basset enthusiasts.

reassured that there is nothing to worry about. If you mollycoddle him and sympathise with him, he is far more likely to retain the memory of his fear.

SENIORITY PERIOD
(12 to 16 weeks)

During this period, your Basset puppy starts to cut the apron strings and becomes more independent. He will test out his status to find out who is the pack leader: him or you. Bad habits, such as play biting, which may have been seen as endearing a few weeks earlier, should be firmly discouraged. Remember to use positive, reward-based training, but make sure your

puppy knows that you are the leader and must be respected.

SECOND FEAR-IMPRINT
PERIOD (6 to 14 months)

This period is not as critical as the first fear-imprint period, but it should still be handled carefully. During this time your Basset Hound may appear apprehensive, or he may show fear of something familiar. You may feel as if you have taken a backwards step, but if you adopt a calm, positive manner, your Basset will see that there is nothing to be frightened of. Do not make your dog confront the thing that frightens him. Simply distract his attention, and give him something else to

think about, such as obeying a simple command, such as "Sit" or "Down". This will give you the opportunity to praise and reward your dog and will help to boost his confidence.

YOUNG ADULTHOOD AND
MATURITY (1 to 4 years)

The timing of this phase depends on the size of the dog: the bigger the dog, the later it is. This period coincides with a dog's increased size and strength, mental as well as physical. Some dogs, particularly those with a dominant nature, will test your leadership again and may become aggressive towards other dogs. Firmness and continued training

TRAINING CLUBS

There are lots of training clubs to choose from. Your vet will probably have details of clubs in your area, or you can ask friends who have dogs if they attend a club. Alternatively, use the internet to find out more information. But how do you know if the club is any good?

Before you take your dog, ask if you can go to a class as an observer and find out the following:
• What experience does the instructor(s) have?
• Do they have experience with Basset Hounds?
• Is the class well organised and are the dogs

reasonably quiet? (A noisy class indicates an unruly atmosphere, which will not be conducive to learning.)
• Are there are a number of classes to suit dogs of different ages and abilities?
• Are positive, reward-based training methods used?
• Does the club train for the Good Citizen Scheme (see page 101)?

If you are not happy with the training club, find another one. An inexperienced instructor who cannot handle a number of dogs in a confined environment can do more harm than good.

are essential at this time, so that your Basset Hound accepts his status in the family pack.

THE ADOLESCENT BASSET HOUND

It happens to every dog – and every owner. One minute you have an obedient well-behaved youngster and the next you have an adolescent who appears to have forgotten everything he ever learnt.

A Basset male will show adolescent behaviour at any time between nine months and 18 months. In terms of behavioural changes, a male may become more sensitive and become frightened by the most innocuous of situations. If this proves to be traumatic and the Basset is not handled correctly, he may develop a life-long phobia.

This is a slow-maturing breed, and a male Basset is not reckoned to be fully mature until he is two or three years old.

Female Basset Hounds mature earlier than males. The age at which a female has her first season is anywhere between six to eleven months; eight to nine months is about usual. If you plan to neuter your bitch, it is far better for her to be allowed to have this season, as she has had more chance to develop properly. A bitch that is spayed before her first season will grow taller than usual and will never mature properly, either in body or mind. Generally, a female Basset will reach maturity at two years of age and become calmer and more 'lady-like' – but they will not be

averse to a skit with a playful puppy.

Adolescence can be a trying time, but it is a transitory phase, which, if handled correctly, will be an important part of the growing-up process. Be firm and consistent so your Basset respects your judgement and is happy to accept you as leader. If a male becomes unduly nervous in a particular situation, do not pander to him or he will start to take himself seriously. Be calm and confident, and try to distract his attention with a treat or a toy, or simply run through a simple training exercise in order to refocus his mind. Do not be

confrontational and force a Basset to face his fears – you will meet with total resistance and will turn a minor incident into a lifelong trauma.

WHEN THINGS GO WRONG

Positive, reward-based training has proved to be the most effective method of teaching dogs, but what happens when your Basset Hound does something wrong and you need to show him that his behaviour is unacceptable? The old-fashioned school of dog training used to rely on the powers of punishment and negative reinforcement. A dog who raided the bin, for example,

An adolescent Basset should be treated firmly but with sensitivity.

Despite your best efforts, you may come up against problem behaviour.

was smacked. Now we have learnt that it is not only unpleasant and cruel to hit a dog, it is also ineffective. If you hit a dog for stealing, he is more than likely to see you as the bad consequence of stealing, so he may raid the bin again, but probably not when you are around. If he raided the bin some time before you discovered it, he will be even more confused by your punishment, as he will not relate your response to his 'crime'.

A more commonplace example is when a dog fails to respond to a recall in the park. Bassets who are always given a food reward when they return, always return – unless they are on a very interesting scent. Then they are deaf and daft! In this instance, when the dog eventually comes back, the owner is tempted to put the dog on the lead and go straight home to punish the dog for his poor response. Unfortunately, the dog will have a different interpretation. He does

not think: "I won't ignore a recall command because the bad consequence is the end of my play in the park." He thinks: "Coming to my owner resulted in the end of playtime – therefore coming to my owner has a bad consequence, so I won't do that again."

There are a number of strategies to tackle undesirable behaviour – and they have nothing to do with harsh handling.

Ignoring bad behaviour: The Basset Hound can be strong-willed when it comes to getting what he wants, and if you are not careful, he will start dictating the rules of the game. For example, a Basset that barks when you are preparing his food is showing his impatience and is attempting to train you, rather than the other way round. He believes he can change a situation simply by making a noise – and even if he does not get his food any quicker, he is enjoying the attention he is getting when you shout at him to tell him to be

quiet. He is still getting attention, so why inhibit his behaviour?

In this situation, the best and most effective response is to ignore your Basset Hound. Suspend food preparations and get on with another task, such as washing up. Do not go near the food or the food bowl again until your Basset is calm and quiet. Repeat this on every occasion when your Basset barks and he will soon learn that barking is non-productive. He is not rewarded with your attention – or with getting food. It will not take long for him to realise that being quiet is the most effective strategy. In this scenario, you have not only taught your Basset Hound to be quiet when you are preparing his food, you have also earned his respect because you have taken control of the situation.

Stopping bad behaviour: There are occasions when you want to call an instant halt to whatever it is your Basset Hound is doing. In most cases, this will be when you have caught him red-handed: for example, raiding the rubbish bin. He has already committed the 'crime', so your aim is to stop him and to redirect his attention. You can do this by clapping your hands once loudly and using a deep, firm tone of voice to say "No".

With some dogs, you can then redirect their focus with a toy or a treat – but not with a Basset. He will always associate the reward with raiding the bin and will think his 'crime' is doubly worthwhile, so you need to adopt a different strategy. Try withdrawing from your dog – just for 10 or 15 minutes – and when you return, you can carry on as normal. A Basset will usually retire to his bed or his crate during this time of separation, and although it is not a direct punishment, he realises he has not won your approval and that is why you have absented yourself. This strategy has been tried with many different Bassets over many generations, and it really does seem to work.

In a more extreme situation, when you want to interrupt undesirable behaviour and you know that a simple "No" will not do the trick, you can try something a little more dramatic. If you get a can and fill it with pebbles, it will make a really loud noise when you shake it or throw it. The same effect can be achieved with purpose-made training discs. The dog will be startled and stop what he is doing. Even better, the dog will not associate the unpleasant noise with you. This gives you the perfect opportunity to be the nice guy, calling the dog to you and giving him lots of praise.

PROBLEM BEHAVIOUR

If you have trained your Basset Hound from puppyhood, survived his adolescence and established yourself as a fair and consistent leader, you will end up with a brilliant companion dog. The Basset is a well-balanced dog who rarely has hang-ups if he has been correctly reared and socialised. Most Basset Hounds are confident, fun-loving and

thrive on spending time with their owners.

However, it may be that you have taken on a rescued Basset Hound that has established behavioural problems, or you may have allowed your Basset too much of a free rein when he was growing up, resulting in undesirable or inappropriate behaviour.

It is never too late to retrain your Basset – even though it may take a lot of time and patience to correct bad habits. But if you are worried about your Basset Hound and feel out of your depth, do not delay in seeking professional help. This is readily available, usually through a referral from your vet, or you can find out additional information on the internet (see Appendices for web addresses). An animal behaviourist will have experience in tackling problem behaviour and will be able to help both you and your dog.

SEPARATION ANXIETY

A Basset Hound loves his human family and may become very distressed – to the point of howling – if he is left alone. This may start the very first night in his new home when he has to cope without the comfort of his littermates and then loses his new-found human friends as everyone disappears to bed. If you go to reassure your puppy in this situation, there is a very good chance that you will end up with a Basset that howls every time he is left on his own.

A puppy should be brought up to accept short periods of separation from his owner so that he does not become anxious. A new puppy should be left for short periods on his own, ideally in his bed in a crate where he cannot get up to any mischief, and where he is used to sleeping overnight.

A boredom-busting toy will provide occupation for your Basset when he is on his own.

RESOURCE GUARDING

If you have trained and socialised your Basset Hound correctly, he will know his place in the family pack and will have no desire to challenge your authority. But if you have taken on a rescued dog who has not been trained and socialised, or if you have allowed your Basset to rule the roost, you may find you have problems with a dog who is continually trying to elevate his status within the family pack.

This behaviour is expressed in many different ways, which may include the following:

- Showing lack of respect for your personal space. For example, your dog will barge through doors ahead of you.
- Ignoring basic obedience commands.
- Showing no respect to younger members of the family, pushing amongst them and completely ignoring them.
- Male dogs may start marking (cocking their leg) in the house.
- Aggression towards people or other dogs (see page 100).

However, the most common behaviour displayed by a Basset Hound who has ideas above his station, is resource guarding. This may take a number of different forms:

- Getting up on to the sofa or your favourite armchair and growling when you tell him to get back on the floor. This will not happen, provided you never let him sit on the furniture in the first place. However, if you take on a rescued Basset, he may have got into bad habits with his previous owners.
- Becoming possessive over a toy or guarding his food bowl by growling when you get too close. Again, this is unlikely to happen unless you have a rescued Basset who has learnt to be assertive in his previous home.

In each of these scenarios, the Basset has something he values and he aims to keep it. He does not have sufficient respect for you, his human leader, to give up what he wants and he is 'warning' you to keep away.

If you see signs of your Basset Hound behaving in this way, you must work at lowering his status so that he realises that you are the leader and he must accept your authority. Although you need to be firm, you also need to use positive training methods so that your Basset is rewarded for the behaviour you want. In this way, his 'correct' behaviour will be strengthened and repeated.

The golden rule is not to become confrontational. The dog will see this as a challenge and may become even more determined not to co-operate. There are a number of steps you can take to lower your Basset Hound's status, which are far more likely to have a successful outcome. They include:

- Go back to basics and hold daily training sessions. Make sure you have some really tasty treats, or find a toy your Basset really values and only bring it out at training sessions. Run through all the training exercises you have taught your Basset. By giving him things to do, you providing mental stimulation and you have the opportunity to make a big fuss of him and reward him when he does well. This will help to reinforce the message that you are the leader and that it is rewarding to do as you ask.
- Teach your Basset something new: this can be as simple as learning a trick, such as shaking paws. Having something new to think about will mentally stimulate your Basset Hound and he will benefit from interacting with you.
- Be 100 per cent consistent with all house rules and make sure that the rest of your family

A Basset may decide that his place is on the sofa...

comply (particularly your children) – your Basset Hound must never sit on the sofa and you must never allow him to jump up at you.

- If your Basset Hound is becoming possessive over toys, remove them all and keep them out of reach. It is then up to you to decide when to produce a toy and to initiate a game. Equally, it is you who will decide when the game is over and when to remove the toy. This teaches your Basset that you 'own' his toys. He has fun playing and interacting with you, but the game is over – and the toy is given up – when you say so.
- If your Basset Hound has been guarding his food bowl, you need to show that you are in charge. Find a chair and sit next to your Basset, holding his bowl. You can then hand feed your dog, making sure he does not jump up or snatch at the food.
- Make sure the family eats before you feed your

Basset Hound. Some trainers advocate eating in front of the dog (maybe just a few bites from a biscuit) before starting a training session, so the dog appreciates your elevated status.
- Do not let your Basset barge through doors ahead of you. You may need to put your dog on the lead and teach him to "Wait" at doorways and then reward him for letting you go through first. It is also useful to teach your Basset a command, such as "Out", to use when you are letting him out into the garden on his own.

If your Basset Hound is progressing well with his retraining programme, think about getting involved with a dog sport, such as agility or tracking. This will give your Basset a positive outlet for his energies. However, if your Basset is still seeking to be dominant, or you have any other concerns, do not delay in seeking the help of an animal behaviourist.

Problems with separation anxiety are most likely to arise if you take on a rescued dog who has major insecurities. You may also find your Basset Hound hates being left if you have failed to accustom him to short periods of isolation when he was growing up. Separation anxiety is expressed in a number of ways and all are equally distressing for both dog and owner. An anxious dog who is left alone may bark, whine or howl continuously; he may urinate and defecate, and may be extremely destructive.

There are a number of steps you can take when attempting to solve this problem:

• Accustom your Basset to sleeping in a crate and leave the crate door open for him to come and go while you are at home. Every time he earns a treat for good behaviour, give him his treats in his crate so he associates the crate with a good place.

• Put up a baby-gate between adjoining rooms and leave your dog in one room while you are in the other room. Your dog will be able to see you and hear you, but he is learning to cope without being right next to you. Build up the amount of time you can leave your dog in easy stages.

• Buy some boredom-busting toys and fill them with some tasty treats. Whenever you leave your dog, give him a food-filled toy so that he is busy while you are away.

• If you have not used a crate before, it is not too late to start. Make sure the crate is cosy and train your Basset to get used to going in his crate while you are in the same room. Gradually build up the amount of time he spends in the crate and then start leaving the room for short periods. When you return, do not make a fuss of your dog. Leave him for five or ten minutes before releasing him, so that he gets used to your comings and goings.

• Pretend to go out, putting on your coat and jangling keys, but do not leave the house. An anxious dog often becomes hyped up by the ritual of leaving and this will help to desensitise him.

• When you go out, leave a radio or a TV switched on. Some dogs are comforted by hearing voices and background noise when they are left alone.

• Try to make your absences as short as possible when you are first training your dog to accept being on his own.

If you take these steps, your dog should become less anxious and, over a period of time, you should be able to solve the problem. However, if you are failing to make progress, do not delay in calling in expert help.

AGGRESSION

Aggression is a complex issue, as there are different causes and the

If you Basset is being possessive over a toy, do a swap with another toy or a treat so it is worth his while to co-operate.

behaviour may be triggered by numerous factors. It may be directed towards people, but far more commonly it is directed towards other dogs. Aggression in dogs may be the result of:

- Assertive behaviour (see 'Resource guarding' page 98).
- Defensive behaviour: This may be induced by fear, pain or punishment.
- Territory: A dog may become aggressive if strange dogs or people enter his territory (which is generally seen as the house and garden).
- Intra-sexual issues: This is aggression between sexes male-to-male or female-to-female.
- Parental instinct: A mother dog may become aggressive if she is protecting her puppies.

Socialising your Basset with dogs of sound temperament will help to prevent aggressive or nervous behaviour.

The Basset Hound is a sociable dog who gets on well with all dogs, and particularly those of his own breed. However, there are instances when a Basset appears to have provoked aggression in another dogs, although there have been no visible signs. It seems that the Basset, in the same way as other canines, has the ability to communicate his feelings – positive or negative – almost telepathically, which results in an unexpected response.

This is more likely to happen if a dog is left on his own and may feel vulnerable or threatened. It has been observed that Basset Hounds left on their show benches for lengthy periods may become increasingly worried, and

this may develop into aggressive behaviour. It is important to bear in mind that if you have taken on the role of leader, you cannot abandon it when something more interesting turns up and leave your Basset to cope in a challenging situation. As discussed, all Bassets should be able to cope for short periods on their own, but this is very different from leaving your dog in an environment where he feels threatened and uncomfortable.

If your Basset appears to have issues with other dogs, you must work at re-educating him so that he observes canine manners and keeps himself out of trouble. The best way to do this is to meet and walk with people who have dogs of sound temperament. Keep the situation low-key and, as far as possible, allow the dogs to communicate and work out their own relationship.

If your Basset is showing

aggressive behaviour in an attempt to elevate his own position in the family, you can try the measures outlined in this chapter. But if you are concerned about your dog's behaviour, you would be well advised to call in professional help. If the aggression is directed towards people, you should seek *immediate* advice. This behaviour can escalate very quickly and could have disastrous consequences.

NEW CHALLENGES
If you enjoy training your Basset Hound, you may want to try one of the many dog sports that are now on offer.

GOOD CITIZEN SCHEME
This is a scheme run by the Kennel Club in the UK and the American Kennel Club in the USA. The schemes promote responsible ownership and help

You may have ambitions to show your Basset.

With careful instruction, a Basset will learn how to negotiate an agility course.

you to train a well-behaved dog who will fit in with the community. The schemes are excellent for all pet owners and they are also a good starting point if you plan to compete with your Basset when he is older. The KC and AKC schemes vary in format. In the UK there is a foundation course, and then bronze, silver and gold awards with each test becoming progressively more demanding. In the AKC scheme there is a single test.

The tests are designed to show the control you have over your dog and his ability to respond correctly and remain calm in all situations. They include walking on a loose lead among people and other dogs and a controlled greeting where dogs stay under control while their owners meet.

The Good Citizen Scheme is taught at most training clubs. For more information, log on to the Kennel Club or AKC website (see Appendices).

SHOWING
Showing is a highly competitive sport and if you take entry fees and travel expenses into account, it can be quite costly. However, many owners get bitten by the showing bug, and their calendar is governed by the dates of the top showing fixtures.

To be successful in the show ring, a Basset must conform as closely as possible to the Breed Standard, which is a written blueprint describing the 'perfect' Basset Hound (see Chapter Seven).

To get started you need to buy a puppy that has show potential and then train him to perform in the ring. Many training clubs hold ringcraft classes, which are run by experienced showgoers. At these classes you will learn how to handle your Basset in the ring, and you will also find out about rules, procedures and show-ring etiquette.

The best plan is to start off at some small, informal shows where you can practise and learn the tricks of the trade before graduating to bigger shows. It's a long haul starting in the very first puppy class, but the dream is to make your Basset into a Champion.

COMPETITIVE OBEDIENCE
The Basset Hound is not a precision breed, and accuracy is not his strong suit. However, there is no doubting his intelligence, and he is more than capable of learning the exercises used in competitive obedience.

There are various levels of achievement, starting with basic obedience exercises and then working up to higher grades with more complex tasks. There are Basset Hound owners who enjoy the challenge – and as long as you (and your trainer) retain a sense of humour, it is enjoyable for both you and your Basset.

Even though competitive obedience requires accuracy and precision, make sure you make it fun for your Basset Hound, with lots of praise and rewards so that you motivate him to do his best. Many training clubs run advanced classes for those who want to compete in obedience, or you can hire the services of a professional trainer for one-on-one sessions.

AGILITY

This fun sport has grown enormously in popularity over the past few years, and although the Basset Hound is not really built for the job, he will enjoy the exercise and the stimulation of taking part. If you fancy having a go, make sure you have good control over your Basset Hound and keep him slim. Agility is a very physical sport, which demands fitness from both dog and handler.

In agility competitions, each dog must complete a set course over a series of obstacles, which include:
- Jumps (upright hurdles and long jump, varying in height – small, medium and large, depending on the size of the dog)

- Weaves
- A-frame
- Dog walk
- Seesaw
- Tunnels (collapsible and rigid)
- Tyre

The winner is the dog that completes the course in the fastest time with no faults. As you progress up the levels, courses become progressively harder.

If you want to get involved in agility, you will need to find an agility club (see Appendices). You will not be allowed to start training until your Basset is 12 months old and you cannot compete until he is 18 months old. This rule is for the protection of the dog, who may suffer injury if he puts strain on bones and joints while he is still growing.

TRACKING
Organised tracking takes place in America and Australia, and Basset Hounds show outstanding ability. For further information see panel on page 104.

SUMMING UP
The Basset Hound is an outstanding companion dog – and once you have owned one, no other breed will do. He is intelligent, fun-loving and affectionate. Make sure you keep

your half of the bargain: spend time socialising and training your Basset Hound so that you can be proud to take him anywhere and he will always be a credit to you.

With a bit of hard work, you will be rewarded with a well-behaved companion that is second to none.

TRACKING TIPS

osemary Izard Corbett grew up in the world of Bassets, and has also spent some time working in Basset kennels in different countries. She first came across tracking in the USA, and gives her own insight into this fascinating aspect of the breed.

"I feel tracking is a very important aspect of the breed and should be regarded as part of the whole. Seeking out scents and following a trail is the purpose and function of our breed and it would be a great disservice to future Basset breeders if this wonderful talent is lost.

"Tracking is one of the most wonderful experiences an owner can have with their hound. Learning to trust your hound's ability is hugely rewarding and lets you enter their world as you learn about their amazing ability.

"Basset Hounds will follow a scent with determination. They become deaf, blind and totally oblivious to an owner's calls, titbits and curses. They are often referred to as being 'stubborn' and this is usually used as a derogatory illustration of our breed! However, the above 'qualities' are what is required of a good tracking hound and become apparent when you place your trust in your trained hound.

"Trust and Bassets are not words that sit comfortably together, and trust of his hound is one of the hardest aspects of tracking for any owner to master. It took me a long time to rely on my hound, having been brought up in a 'show' environment where a mere flick of your wrist can control your show dog's movement. Tracking is the opposite of this tight control; your involvement in the activity is merely to hold the 40ft-long tracking line. The temptation to correct your hound when he veers off course is almost unbearable, but the slightest movement of your hound will lose him points in competition.

"Teaching your hound to track is relatively easy and inexpensive; our team use the following items when training hounds. All are vital for training your hound:

A glove or shoe: This is the prize your hound must find at the end of the track. It is not necessary for him to retrieve this and return it to you – just to find the article.

Bamboo canes: These are for you to use as a training aid, mark the progress and ensure your hound is following a precisely laid-out track. In competition there will be no bamboo canes.

Shoulder harness: To fit your hound. This can be as expensive or as cheap as you want – but it must be comfortable, well fitting and adjustable (your hound may gain or lose weight). The harness must be fitted with a ring where the tracking line will be attached.

Nylon line: A 40ft (12-metre) nylon line needs to have a lead clip attached to the end, which can then be attached to your hound's harness.

Spreadable processed cheese: This is a firm favourite with Bassets and one that is used worldwide in training. I have tried many different scents and always came back to cheese! The first time I tried it, I was so lacking in confidence that I spread almost the whole tube in laying the track, which my hounds thought was wonderful as they lapped up the cheese – very little scenting went on in that first session… The purpose of using this type of cheese is to smear a very small amount on the soles of your tracking shoes, which helps your hound to pick up a scent. The cheese is easy to apply to the soles and can be stored in a pocket.

Strong scented treats: This can be anything your hound finds really tasty and thoroughly enjoys, but it must have a strong smell so your hound builds up an association and the same treat must be used on all occasions.

"If you have a large garden, then the initial training can begin there – an empty field is even better. I usually place the bamboo canes 50 paces apart and, to start with, these are usually in a straight line of four or five bamboo canes.

"When I first started tracking, I usually chose good weather, as I felt my hounds would be unable to pick up a scent in wet weather conditions. I discovered this was a mistake, as dry, sunny conditions evaporate the track much faster than in wet or damp conditions, which keep the scent grounded.

"The wind must never be blowing into your hound's face (downwind) and should preferably be behind you and your dog. Having the breeze blowing towards you could teach your hound to pick up the scent from the wind and not put his nose to the track. I have one character who steadfastly refuses to scent the grass and smells his treat on the breeze and runs straight to the first bait. This is the primary sin in tracking and is very difficult to break.

"Motivation is the key tool in tracking during the initial stages, as your hound has to be taught how to track in a straight line, not to veer off and not to 'round' on the scent. At this stage your hound can become a little bored, but if the correct motivation has been in place from the beginning, it should not be a problem. Short positive words inducing alertness in your hound are advisable: for example, "Let's go track", said in the same tone and used only when tracking begins, will be suitable encouragement.

"I have tried many different scents; I was convinced that tripe would do the trick but, after several trays of tripe were trodden in and scraped on to the track, I went back to the processed cheese, which was less messy, easier to control and could be kept sealed out of the tracking zone, and away from thieving hounds…

"A small amount of the cheese can be rubbed on to the soles the tracklayer's shoe; he or she then shuffles around the course, laying a little of the cheesy scent trail from the shoes.

"A treat is also left at each marker during the training (to encourage the Hound) – though for an actual competition, there are no markers and so the dog only gets a treat at the end of the line. Initially, start with a fairly small track, placing bamboo cane markers at regular intervals. I usually start my training track with the markers at 50 paces apart. To do this, wear different shoes to the tracking (always keep to the same shoes for laying a scent). Once you have laid out all your markers and reached the end of your track, double back down your original lines.

"At the start line encourage your hound to locate the correct track; after a few hounds have 'worked' a track, it will become stale and the scent of other hounds and owners could confuse your hound. Motivate your hound, and then let him work.

"Allow a certain amount of your tracking lead out until your hound becomes fixated on the scent, and then gradually let out your lead and follow your hound.

"Follow your hound to the first marker and allow him to eat his treat and then motivate him again with your chosen phrase. Repeat the process until the end of the track is reached where your glove or shoe will have been left with a treat on top."

THE PERFECT BASSET HOUND

Chapter 7

Despite an apt description of the breed in Shakespeare's *Midsummer Night's Dream*, it is doubtful that today's Basset Hound would be recognised as being the same as the dwarfed hounds of Shakespeare's time. Early breeders crossbred without compunction if they thought they could improve a characteristic they considered important.

The Basset Hound has, undoubtedly, been developed from French Hounds – the now extinct Basset Artois (a large, heavily-made hound on short legs); the Basset Bleu de Gascogne (a rather large, but not too heavy, hound with mottled coat and ample skin) and the Basset Artesian Norman (a long dog, longer than its size calls for,

with crooked forelegs) – and the Bloodhound.

The term 'Basset' is a descriptive word that comes from the French word 'bas', meaning low or dwarfed. In France, the hound breed name includes the region of origin to denote the main hunting area associated with that breed. For example, the Basset Griffon Vendeen hunted in the Vendee regions; the Basset Fauve de Bretagne hunted in Brittany, and the Basset Bleu de Gascogne comes from the ancient province of Gascony in southern France.

THE BREED STANDARDS

Although the Basset Hound has evolved from a number of French hounds, the French recognise that 'le Basset Hound' evolved in the British Isles and give the country of origin as Grande Bretagne. The majority of the European

countries are affiliated to the FCI (Fédération Cynologique Internationale), which also recognises the country of origin as being Great Britain and consequently use the British Standard.

The American Standard differs somewhat in the wording, but Bassets bred to the American Breed Standard look very little different to a Basset bred to the British Breed Standard. However, there is a difference in the ring presentation. American dogs are shown with the hind feet set further back than the point of buttock in order to accentuate the hind angulation; and the head is held straight upwards in order to accentuate the length of neck and demonstrate the extent of the prosternum.

The Kennel Club Breed Standard was revised in 2009. The eight

BASSET CHAMPIONS

Multi Ch. Bellecombe Eugenie. Bred and owned by Grace Servais (Switzerland).

Am. Ch. Showtime's Shock and Awe: Basset Hound Club of America National Specialty Best of Breed winner 2008.
Breeders/co-owners: Howard and Barbara Haskell, Mark and Sandi Chryssanthis, and Chris Wallen.
Photographer: Nugent.

UK breed clubs met to discuss a number of changes. The agreed changes were considered by the Kennel Club and, in the summer of 2009, judges and show societies were ssued with the new text (below).

The most radical change was the addition of an introductory paragraph, which has the same wording for every breed recognised by the British Kennel Club:

A Breed Standard is the guideline which describes the ideal characteristics, temperament and appearance of a breed and ensures that the breed is fit for function. Absolute soundness is essential. Breeders and judges should at all times be careful to avoid obvious conditions or exaggerations which would be detrimental in any way to the health, welfare or soundness of this breed. From time to time certain conditions or exaggerations may be considered to have the potential to affect dogs in some breeds adversely, and judges and breeders are requested to refer to the Kennel Club website for details of any such current issues. If a feature or quality is desirable, it should only be present in the right measure.

The phrase: "Absolute soundness is essential" is of paramount importance. Soundness can refer to the physical appearance of the dog – the bone structure, skin, feet, eyes, ears, mouth, etc. – all being in the correct proportions. Conformation problems may arise when too much emphasis is placed on a specific breed point; breed type may also be changed.

For some years leading up to 2009 and the subsequent changes to the UK Standard, it appeared that an increasingly large number of breeders and judges, worldwide, were of the opinion that "...if some is good, then more must be better..." A short-legged hound of considerable substance became an 'ultra short-legged' hound of excess substance. A Basset Hound should have the substance comparable to that of the working Labrador, for example.

Judges were giving awards to very short legs. Consequently, breeders were breeding for that prize feature. The leg length shortened, and shortened again – so that when standing in slightly long grass, sometimes the legs could not be seen. The Basset Hound is a dwarf; it should have the body length of a normal dog and shortened limbs (not *ultra* short limbs – just shortened). It is hoped the 2009 changes to the Breed Standard will redress the problem of too short a limb length.

Many non-specialist judges – and a few specialist judges – try to judge the Basset Hound using a similar height-to-length ratio as for a 'normal' dog. Unfortunately, along with too short legs, we have had Bassets who are too short in body to make it appear more in proportion to leg length. It is in this way that breed type changes.

The term 'soundness' conveys the sense of a lack of exaggeration and of a dog in total balance of all points – breed and conformation.

It is essential that the Basset retains the conformation that allows him to perform his original function as a scent hound.

A sound dog is a healthy dog. Soundness is not only important in body, it is of equal importance in the mind. A dog of sound temperament is a dog who is neither too shy nor too bold, neither fearful nor aggressive.

At the time of writing, the specific changes to the Breed Standard in 2009 have had little effect on the breed. Some, few, judges are conscientiously awarding prizes to dogs with slightly longer limbs and less loose skin. It will take time and a number of generations for the breed to look as agile as it did in the 1970s, when many dogs were still hunted in the Basset packs.

ANALYSIS AND INTERPRETATION

The Kennel Club (KC) Breed Standard is reproduced alongside the American Kennel Club (AKC) Breed Standard, followed by a detailed analysis of the two Standards.

GENERAL APPEARANCE AND CHARACTERISTICS

KC

Short-legged hound of considerable substance, well balanced, full of quality. It is important to bear in mind that this is a working hound and must be fit for purpose, therefore should be strong, active and capable of great endurance in the field. Characteristics: A tenacious hound of ancient lineage which hunts by scent, possessing a pack instinct and a deep melodious voice.

AKC

The Basset Hound possesses in marked degree those characteristics which equip it admirably to follow a trail over and through difficult terrain. It is a short-legged dog, heavier in bone, size considered, than any other breed of dog, and while its movement is deliberate, it is in no sense clumsy.

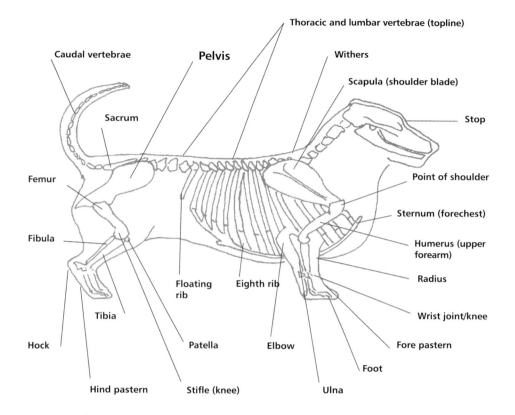

Caudal vertebrae

Pelvis

Thoracic and lumbar vertebrae (topline)

Withers

Scapula (shoulder blade)

Stop

Sacrum

Point of shoulder

Femur

Sternum (forechest)

Fibula

Humerus (upper forearm)

Radius

Floating rib

Eighth rib

Wrist joint/knee

Tibia

Fore pastern

Hock

Patella

Elbow

Foot

Hind pastern

Stifle (knee)

Ulna

Points of the skeleton: It is useful to have some knowledge of the skeletal structure when considering a Basset's conformation.

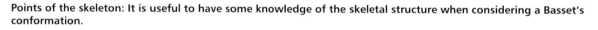

"Considerable substance"
A Basset Hound with long legs, like a Labrador or Dalmatian, will look no more substantial than any other breed. It is the mere fact that there is more body than leg that gives the appearance of 'considerable'. Substance must be equated with tight muscles laid over strong healthy bone – not overweight and flabby muscle over weak small bones.

"Heavier in bone, size considered"
The actual bone is no 'heavier' than in a standard-height hound

(of a non-dwarf breed), i.e. Foxhound; but it is certainly stronger and thicker than that of a non-dwarf breed of dog that stands '*around*' 14 inches at the shoulder - such as a Beagle.

"A working hound"
Since the UK Hunting Acts came into force in 2004, very few Kennel Club-registered Basset Hounds have been 'worked' in packs in Great Britain; although some packs are still in existence and are registered with the Masters of Hounds, where they follow a laid

trail. However, it is essential that the breed does retain the stamina and ability to be fit for purpose. Field trials, organised tracking and 'scenting days' are ways of ensuring this. In some countries, hounds may not become a full Champion until they have gained a working or tracking certificate.

"Ancient lineage"
This is rather wishful thinking (see Chapter Two: The First Basset Hounds). However, this breed has been developed from scent hounds and the various Basset

'types' that have been 'hunted' so successfully for centuries.

"Deep melodious voice" and "endurance in the field"

If a Basset 'takes off' after a particularly interesting scent, the "deep melodious voice" (KC) well used, can often be heard and "the endurance in the field" (AKC) can be well demonstrated to the frustrated owner, who is probably at least two (or three) fields away.

A Basset out for a normal country walk will need gates opening, will need lifting across a ditch, and could not possibly push through a hedge. A Basset on a strong scent will negotiate all three without noticing!

TEMPERAMENT
KC
Placid, never aggressive or timid. Affectionate.

AKC
In temperament it is mild, never sharp or timid. It is capable of great endurance in the field and is extreme in its devotion.

In temperament the Basset Hound is calm and placid - unless he sees his lead and knows he is going for a walk and then he is liable to become quite excitable. He is normally a gentle 'person' and copes with strange events without fear or aggression - though possibly a little bewilderment (and he may look up at you as if to say, "Did you see that?" or, "What was that about?"). He is very affectionate and has a strong devotion to his

'pack' (which might include the family cat or another dog) and the extended family of humans.

A pedigree is a list of ancestors, and is reliant on the trust and honesty of the person who writes it – it is no guarantee of good temperament.

A reputable breeder will carefully select the right mate and will breed for good temperament. A puppy farmer, puppy mill or 'cash crop' breeder is not interested in selecting the right mate, only in acquiring a good return on his investment. Unfortunately, a Kennel Club registration is no guarantee of a good, well-bred puppy.

Like any other breed, the first few days in the new home are crucial. The ground rules must be set and adhered to. If a puppy is

The head is domed – a broad flat skull is considered a fault.

always being shouted at, instead of shown what to do, he will become timid. If a puppy is teased, he will become fractious and possibly aggressive.

Love has to be given as well as taken; a quiet word of praise with a gentle stroke conveys more affection to the dog than him being frequently picked up and carried and cuddled.

HEAD AND SKULL
KC
Domed with some stop and occipital bone prominent; of medium width at brow and tapering slightly to muzzle; general appearance of foreface lean not snipey. Top of muzzle nearly parallel with line from stop to occiput and not much longer than head from stop to occiput. There may be a small amount of wrinkle at brow and beside eyes. In any event skin of head supple enough as to wrinkle slightly when drawn forward or when head is lowered. Flews of upper lip overlap lower substantially. Nose entirely black except in light-coloured hounds when it may be brown or liver. Large and well opened nostrils may protrude a little beyond lips.

AKC
The head is large and well proportioned. Its length from occiput to muzzle is greater than the width at the brow. In overall appearance the head is of medium width. The *skull* is well domed, showing a pronounced occipital

The Basset has a calm, serious expression.

protuberance. A broad flat skull is a fault. The length from nose to stop is approximately the length from stop to occiput. The sides are flat and free from cheek bumps. Viewed in profile the top lines of the muzzle and skull are straight and lie in parallel planes, with a moderately defined stop. The skin over the whole of the head is loose, falling in distinct wrinkles over the brow when the head is lowered. A dry head and tight skin are faults. The *muzzle* is deep, heavy, and free from snipiness. The *nose* is darkly pigmented, preferably black, with large wide-open nostrils. A deep liver-colored nose conforming to the coloring of the head is permissible but not desirable. The *lips* are darkly pigmented and are pendulous, falling squarely in

front and, toward the back, in loose hanging flews.

How to explain the head to someone who might never have looked closely at a Basset…
The head is of medium width with a prominent occiput. However, compared to some breeds it could be considered quite narrow, so it must be considered in proportion to the whole hound. Broad, flat heads are described as 'coarse'.

Gently hold a Basset head, with thumbs on the top of the ears; you will see the skull is somewhat longer than wide and at the back of the skull there is a slight bump – the occiput – which serves as an area for muscle attachment.

At the eyebrows, there may be a *little* loose skin sufficient to form a wrinkle, but not so much as to pull the eyebrows downwards.

Loose skin should give noticeable wrinkle when pulled forward; a small amount of loose skin is desirable but an excessive amount will pull down a loose eye and show considerable 'haw' (i.e. the inner side of the eyelid - thus exposing a large amount of the red conjunctival lining - see eyes) – this is *not* desirable. However, a head with no loose skin at all appears very plain and is said to be 'dry'.

The stop – the area between the eyes – slopes slightly down to the muzzle; it is not a definite 'step'. From the eyes, the face gradually narrows towards the nose. The cheeks are flat and smooth, not prominent, and may carry some wrinkles when the head is facing downwards.

With the KC Standard, the foreface (muzzle) will be *nearly* parallel to the skull (a Roman nose is not at all unusual) and, whilst not being of equal length to the skull, should not be much longer.

The AKC Standard asks for the foreface and skull to lie in parallel planes - but considering the ancestry of the breed, the slightly aquiline foreface of the Basset Bleu de Gascogne is quite occasionally apparent and should not be considered a fault.

A weak or pointed foreface is considered 'snipy' and is not acceptable.

KC "Flews of upper lip overlap lower substantially"
AKC "… falling squarely in front and, toward the back, in loose hanging flews"

The fleshy, slightly pendulous upper lips hang over the lower jaw. These are the flews and, ideally, will be square to the face rather than sloping backwards from the nose.

The nose may protrude slightly and should be black or it may shade to brown in light-coloured hounds. Unpigmented areas (referred to as a 'butterfly' nose) are a defect but must be assessed against the qualities of the whole dog; it is fairly common in young puppies but usually does eventually fill-in. A butterfly nose will not affect the scenting ability, the main point being that the nostrils are wide and open sufficiently to take in the slightest of scents.

EYES
KC

Lozenge-shaped neither prominent nor deep-set, dark but may shade to mid-brown in light coloured hounds. Expression calm and serious. Light or yellow eye highly undesirable.

AKC

The *eyes* are soft, sad, and slightly sunken, showing a prominent haw, and in color are brown, dark brown preferred. A somewhat lighter-colored eye conforming to the general coloring of the dog is acceptable but not desirable. Very light or protruding eyes are faults.

When measured, the ear leathers should reach slightly beyond the end of the muzzle.

"Lozenge-shaped"
The shape of the eye itself is a normal, round shape – as is the human eye – it is the 'rim', the upper and lower eyelid, which gives the lozenge shape, similar to a flat, wide diamond with all rounded corners.

The rims of the upper or lower eyelid should not turn inwards towards the eyeball (causing the eyelashes to rub against the eye), nor should the lower eyelid be so exceedingly loose as to roll outwards, exposing a large amount of conjunctival membrane (*see 'haw' in above paragraph - 'How to explain the head'*).

The nictitating membrane (often called the 'third' eyelid) at the inner corner of the eye can sometimes become prolapsed

(slip out of place and become well exposed) and this is often known as a 'cherry eye'. The membrane aids in keeping the eyeball moist and clean, and when a large part is exposed to the air, it can become dry and quite uncomfortable.

The American Standard describes the eye as soft and sad - but be assured that when a happy Basset is playing a 'joke' - then they are sparkling, laughing eyes!

In colour, the eyes should be as dark as possible – even in lighter-coloured hounds though it is acceptable to shade to hazel in light-coloured hounds. One or both eyes of blue or white, however, is not acceptable. Blue/white eyes are suspected, though not proven, to be from a puppy farm mis-mating and naive new owners are assured that it is 'special', but it is a genetic fault.

EARS
KC

Set on low, just below line of eye. Long, reaching only slightly beyond end of muzzle of correct length, but not excessively so. Narrow throughout their length and curling well inwards; very supple, fine and velvety in texture.

AKC

The ears are extremely long, low set, and when drawn forward, fold well over the end of the nose. They are velvety in texture, hanging in loose folds

with the ends curling slightly inward. They are set far back on the head at the base of the skull and, in repose, appear to be set on the neck. A high set or flat ear is a serious fault.

KC "Set on low", AKC "low set"
Place your thumbs gently on the top of the ears, and you will note the top of the ear is just below the line of the eye and is normally set well back on the skull, just about below the occiput. However, when your Basset is interested (or playing jokes!) he will lift the top of the ear and bring the leather forward.

Ear leathers should be narrow, long, soft and supple with an inward curl. Thick ears are flat looking, they tend to lose most of the inward curl and are not at all attractive but, importantly, thick, flat ear leathers cannot do such a proper job when the hound is working, as they tend to fall away from the foreface. As the Basset lowers his head to the ground, the faint moisture of his breath will lift the scent; the ear leather helps stir and contain the very faintest of the scent particles – and the hound is off!

The UK and the American Standards differ considerably as to what constitutes a good ear leather. The UK Standard asks for the ear leather to reach *slightly* beyond the end of the muzzle and the American Standard asks for an *extremely long* ear leather, which will fold well over the end of the nose. 'Working' Bassets tend towards the shorter ear leather, which *only just* reaches

beyond the nose. Too long a leather dragging along the ground will stir debris, the smell of which could mask the prey scent - there is also the danger that the hound may step on its own ear and tear the leather or trip over it for another injury.

MOUTH
KC
Jaws strong, with a perfect, regular and complete scissor bite, i.e. upper teeth closely overlapping lower teeth and set square to the jaws.

AKC
The *teeth* are large, sound, and regular, meeting in either a scissors or an even bite. A bite either overshot or undershot is a serious fault.

"Jaws strong"
Absolutely essential with a hunting breed, even if that particular hound will never hunt! Not only should the jaws be strong enough to make an

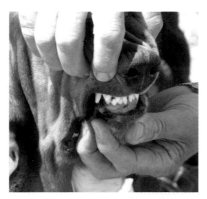
The jaws are strong with a scissor bite.

efficient and quick kill of heavy prey, they should be of sufficient strength to make a clean kill without the jaw breaking whilst doing so.

"Scissor bite"
The 'bite' is the name given to the position of the upper and lower teeth in relation to each other when the mouth is closed.

The most efficient bite for a dog is the scissor bite – the top teeth 'hang' in front of the bottom teeth and closely overlap the bottom teeth – in the same way as is best for ourselves. There should be no gap between them; consider the usefulness of a pair of scissors with a gap between the blades.

A level, or even, bite is when the upper and lower teeth sit directly edge to edge; this will cause wear on the enamel and does not properly grip the prey at the point of capture - it could wriggle free and escape. (A level bite for the Basset Hound is acceptable in the American Standard but not the British Standard, although it *was* acceptable in early Standards.)

A *reverse scissor bite* is where the lower jaw is somewhat longer than the upper jaw so the 'inside' part of the bottom teeth sit in front of the 'outside' part of the top teeth. This is acceptable in some breeds (such as a Pug) but not for the Basset Hound.

An *undershot* mouth is where the lower jaw is longer than the upper jaw and there is a definite gap between the teeth. An *overshot* mouth (sometimes known as a parrot mouth) is where the upper teeth sit well forward of the lower teeth. With a gap between the upper and lower teeth of any hunter, including the Basset Hound, it would be fairly easy for the prey animal to pull free - despite damage to its skin.

A *wry* mouth is caused by an uneven growth pattern causing the lower jaw to twist very slightly to one side, resulting in a misalignment of the teeth. This is not acceptable.

The bones of the lower jaw are the last to stop growing, generally at about three years of age for a medium to large breed such as the Basset Hound.

NECK
KC
Muscular, well arched and fairly long with pronounced but not exaggerated dewlap.

AKC
The **dewlap** is very pronounced. The **neck** is powerful, of good length, and well arched.

This is a scent hound and consequently the neck must be long and muscular and **strong** enough to allow the hound to keep the head comfortably to the scent for long periods. The arch of the neck is controlled by the neck muscles and this is where the strength lies - in the well-developed musculature.

KC "not exaggerated dewlap" versus AKC "the dewlap is very pronounced"
The 'dewlap' is the loose

pendulous skin from the neck and throat of the dog. It should be there; it should be obvious. However, this should not be so excessive and so heavy as to hang down to give a false front or to flap and bounce like a loose bosom when the hound is running - this is both tiresome and tiring.

The dewlap will work with the long ear leathers to move the slightest trace of scent to the nose. Too much dewlap becomes sweaty and encourages bacterial/yeast growth - which brings its own odour and could mask any slight scent of the prey.

FOREQUARTERS
KC
Shoulder blades well laid back; shoulders not heavy. Forelegs short, powerful and with great bone; elbows turning neither in nor out but fitting neatly against side. Upper forearm inclined slightly inwards, but not to such an extent as to prevent free action or to result in legs touching each other when standing or in action; forechest fitting neatly into crook when viewed from front. Knuckling-over highly undesirable. Some wrinkles of skin may appear on lower legs, but this must on no account be excessive.

AKC
The *chest* is deep and full with prominent sternum

showing clearly in front of the legs. The *shoulders* and elbows are set close against the sides of the chest. The distance from the deepest point of the chest to the ground, while it must be adequate to allow free movement when working in the field, is not to be more than one-third the total height at the withers of an adult Basset. The shoulders are well laid back and powerful. Steepness in shoulder, fiddle fronts, and elbows that are out, are serious faults. The *forelegs* are short,

The front legs are short and powerful.

powerful, heavy in bone, with wrinkled skin. Knuckling over of the front legs is a disqualification.

Sometimes referred to as the front assembly, the forequarters take the full weight of the dog during movement – shoulders must *never* be considered alone. They must be in equal balance with the hindquarters. One of the consequences of shoulder angulation not being equal to the hind angulation will be that the hound will have to expend extra energy and flip up the fore foot (padding) or flip the foot slightly outwards (winging) to ensure the footfall is equal front and back.

KC, AKC "well laid back"
The shoulder blades are long and broad and are set at about a 45-degree angle sloping backwards from the point of shoulder and upwards to the withers.

KC "not heavy"
This can relate to a 'loaded' shoulder, with an excess of muscle, or fat, either on the outside and/or under the shoulder blade, giving a lumpy, overdeveloped appearance. Such over-development can lead to a restricted, muscle-bound movement.

AKC "steepness in shoulder is a serious fault"
If the shoulders are too steep, i.e. too upright, the hound loses 'front', i.e. prosternum (that portion of the breastbone which projects beyond the point of shoulder); the neck looks short

and the dog appears unbalanced.

AKC "elbows that are out are a serious fault"
The elbows should lie close to the ribs and should move freely, giving sufficient length of forward reach in order to retain balance during movement. The bone of the upper arm (humerus) should typically be the same length as the shoulder blade (scapula). A short upper arm does not give sufficient length of forward reach and the dog will have to take shorter strides, putting his foot down before the true point of balance. This will give him a choppy front movement with a slight 'roll' from side to side as he moves.

Just for fun, walk quickly along a straight line, with strides of normal length, and note that your feet are placed close towards the straight line. Then attempt the same exercise, but taking much shorter strides. You will have a tendency to waddle and will see that your feet fall further away from the inward straight line.

To allow full forward extension of the front leg during movement, the ideal angle between the upper arm and the shoulder blade is 90 degrees.

The upper arm (humerus) joins the bones of the foreleg (radius and ulna) at the elbow joint. It is these two bones that are particularly susceptible to growth plate damage (see Chapter Five: The Best of Care).

Looking straight at the front of the Basset Hound, the forelegs inclining slightly inwards (referred to as the crook) give stability to

the stance and movement; by bringing the feet under the heaviest part of the body, the elbows should lie smoothly against the sides. The American Standard says that 'fiddle fronts' and elbows that are 'out' are serious faults. A 'fiddle front' is one in which the elbows are rather wide apart, the forearms slope in towards the centre front and the pasterns and feet turn outwards.

When seen in profile, the forelegs appear almost straight and must not, on any account, bend forward at the wrist joint. This is known as "knuckling over", which indicates great unsoundness.

There should be a slight slope to the front pastern (sloping from the foot backwards towards the knee). An upright pastern will cause the dog to 'knuckle' and, in trying to keep the leg straight, extra strain is put on the muscles.

Because this is a large dog with short leg bones, growth-plate injuries are common, particularly in 'pet' Bassets, and can result in one foot (or both) turning outwards – sometimes quite considerably – again, putting extra strain on the muscles.

BODY
One point of great importance that appears in the American Standard and which is omitted in the British Standard is:

"The distance from the deepest point of the chest to the ground, while it must be adequate to

There should be adequate clearance between the lowest point of the chest and the ground.

allow free movement when working in the field, is not to be more than one-third the total height at the withers of an adult Basset."

Ideally, this paragraph should have the addition of "or less" - so as to read: "is not to be more, **or less**, than one-third the total height at the withers..." This is the ratio judges should bear in mind while assessing Basset Hounds.

KC
Long and deep throughout length, breast bone prominent but chest neither narrow nor unduly deep. There should be adequate clearance between the lowest part of the chest and the ground to allow the hound to move freely over all types of terrain. Ribs well rounded and sprung, without flange, extending well back. Back rather broad and level. Withers and quarters of approximately same height, though loins may arch slightly. Back from withers to onset of quarters not unduly long.

AKC
The rib structure is long, smooth, and extends well back. The ribs are well sprung, allowing adequate room for heart and lungs. Flat sidedness and flanged ribs are faults. The topline is straight, level, and free from any tendency to sag or roach, which are faults.

With reference to the American clause above - relating to the deepest point of chest and free movement - it must be remembered this is a normal-sized dog with an abnormal leg length. Therefore, the body needs to be of the same proportions as we expect to find in any other breed, but with certain modifications. Whereas a normal-sized dog would have his elbows set just below the ribcage, in an achondroplastic dog, the elbows lie against the side of the ribs. Consequently, there is a very slight flattening of the ribcage to accommodate the elbow and to allow for a comfortable stance and free movement. An excessive spring of rib can cause the elbow to stick out, particularly when moving, thus causing muscle strain and lack of endurance.

Basically, the shape of the ribs should be similar to the shape of a hen's egg standing on the 'pointed' end.

"Ribs well rounded and sprung"
The spring of rib is the manner in which the ribs emerge from their articulation with the backbone. Spring of rib has a direct influence on heart and lung room and, consequently, on stamina. Ribs that begin to arch soon after emergence will give a barrelled rib, which tends to bring the brisket higher, so losing heart and lung room. Ribs with very little arch will give a flatter ribcage, often described as being slab sided ('flat sided' in the American Standard); this also loses heart and lung room. The brisket, the lowest part of the sternum, should extend backwards beyond the elbows to be 'carried well back'. This is the attachment for the other end of ribs; if the dog has too short a brisket, the dog will be 'herring gutted' and, again, lack stamina.

"Without flange"
The first eight ribs on each side are attached to the sternum by cartilage; the cartilage of the ninth rib is attached to that of the eighth rib where it joins the sternum. It is a slight misalignment of the ninth rib cartilage that will cause the cartilage of the tenth, eleventh

and twelfth ribs (which are joined to the cartilage of the ninth rib) - to lie outwards, thus giving the appearance of a flange. It is very unsightly, as well as considered as not giving absolute 100 per cent protection to the internal organs. The thirteenth rib, the floating rib, can sometimes be felt - this should not be mistaken for a flanged rib.

The withers, i.e. top of the shoulder blades, should be about the same height as the onset of quarters, i.e. the pelvis. The loin is the area between the ribcage and the pelvis. The slight arch required here gives strength to the back, in the same manner that an old-fashioned arched stone bridge will support a heavy load - and the appearance of an arch here is caused by muscle development. It should not be confused with a 'roached' back, which is a fault and is caused by

The hocks are well let down.

a slightly abnormal vertebral contour of the spine. A sagging back speaks for itself; it is weak and unsightly.

The length of body should be dictated by the ribcage, not the loin.

When purchasing a puppy, consider the distance between the end of the ribs and the pelvis in both the puppy and his mother. If this distance is long, then it is more likely that the dog will suffer from back problems.

HINDQUARTERS
KC
Full of muscle and standing out well, giving an almost spherical effect when viewed from rear. Stifles well bent. Hocks well let down and slightly bent under but turn neither in nor out and just under body when standing naturally. Some wrinkles of skin may appear between hock and foot, and at rear of joint a slight pouch of skin may be present, but on no account should any of these be excessive.

AKC
The hindquarters are very full and well rounded, and are approximately equal to the shoulders in width. They must not appear slack or light in relation to the over-all depth of the body. The dog stands firmly on its hind legs showing a well-let-down stifle with no tendency toward a crouching stance. Viewed from behind, the hind legs are parallel, with the hocks turning neither in nor out.

Cowhocks or bowed legs are serious faults. Steep, poorly angulated hindquarters are a serious fault. The dewclaws, if any, may be removed.

Hindquarters must *never* be considered alone. They must be in equal balance with the shoulder angulation in order to give the same push from behind as reach in the front.

The slope of the pelvis, the angle with the upper thigh and the relationship with the lower thigh are all equally important.

Unless the dog has equal angulation front and back, one end has more power than the other and the dog must make a compensation movement – expending extra effort to ensure that the feet hit the ground in the right sequence.

The hindquarters should be muscular with well-bent knee joints, i.e. the stifle. The meaning of '*hocks well let down*' is that the rear pasterns are short (as are the fore pasterns); it does not mean that the pouch of skin, actually on the hock joint, should be heavy and hanging down. The pouch of skin, in fact, serves no real purpose – it is simply loose skin - and should be '*some*', not '*more*' so as to be excessive. Remember here - if "some is good" then more is *definitely not* better.

Standing behind the dog and looking from the rear, the hind feet should point forwards and the hock should neither point towards each other, nor away from each other - they should

appear parallel. The stifle joint should point straight forwards not outwards - this also can be noted from the rear examination.

The 'apple bottom' mentioned in some books (and critiques), but which does not appear in either Standard, is a reminder that the buttocks should be rounded and well muscled and, looking from the rear, one should be reminded of a round, rosy apple with the tail standing up as though it were the stalk!

FEET
KC

Large, well knuckled up and padded. Forefeet may point straight ahead or be turned slightly outwards but in every case the hound always stands perfectly true, weight being born equally by toes with pads together so that feet would leave an imprint of a large hound and no unpadded areas in contact with ground.

The foot is large and well knuckled.

AKC

The paw is massive, very heavy with tough heavy pads, well rounded and with both front feet inclined equally a trifle outward, balancing the width of the shoulders. Feet down at the pastern are a serious fault. The toes are neither pinched together nor splayed, with the weight of the forepart of the body borne evenly on each. The hind feet point straight ahead. The dewclaws may be removed.

The feet are in proportion to the body size not the leg length and so can appear quite massive. The foot is round and compact with the two centre toes being only very slightly longer than the outer toes. The toes are well arched so as to appear '*well knuckled*'; they should appear to be tight - though not so tight as to appear pinched together. The toes should appear well bunched rather than loose and set apart from each other (*splayed*). The toes need to be strong to grip the ground when running.

"*Well… padded*" and "*tough heavy pads*"
The toe pads and centre foot pad should be tough and heavy - deeply cushioned and covered with thick skin. A hound walking on a flat, thin pad is akin to a hiker setting off to walk a long trail in his carpet slippers.

"*Forefeet may point straight ahead or be turned slightly outwards*"
A slight turn outwards keeps the elbows close to the body and so

In the show ring the Basset is stacked and his ta is held in position

will put less strain on the upper arm and shoulders. A dog may be 'stacked' by the handler to show the forefeet pointing straight ahead, but when the dog moves, in order to retain comfort and balance, the feet may point slightly outwards.

If the feet do turn outwards, it must be no more than as 'five minutes to one', as shown on a clock face, otherwise there is undue strain on the leg muscles.

"Feet down at the pastern are a serious fault"
Excessively sloping, or broken down pasterns, reduce exercise tolerance as dogs lose 'spring' in the step and tire more easily. Not good for a working hound!

There is no mention of toenails in either Breed Standard, but the nails should be short. Long nails touching the ground will affect the balance during movement, possibly turning the toes to one side and making the dog walk on the wrong part of the foot, thus putting strain on the leg and corresponding muscles.

TAIL (STERN)
KC
Well set on, rather long, strong at base, tapering, with moderate amount of coarse hair underneath. When moving, stern carried well up and curving gently, sabre-fashion, never curling or gay.

AKC
The tail is not to be docked, and is set in continuation of the spine with but slight curvature, and carried gaily in hound fashion. The hair on the underside of the tail is coarse.

"Well set on"
The musculature over the rump determines the 'tail set' - too much muscle and the tail appears to be set low, whereas insufficient muscle and the tail appears to be set high on the body.

"Strong at base" and *"in continuation of the spine"*
The tail is the *final* portion of the spine. The tail is thicker at the base where it joins the body and

tapers to a point as the caudal vertebrae become smaller. There should be no lumps or kinks within the span, just as there should be none throughout the whole extent of the spine.

KC "…carried well up… sabre-fashion"
AKC".. carried gaily in hound fashion"
(There is quite a difference here between UK terminology and American terminology.)

During movement, the tail should be carried upwards in a gentle curve, reminiscent of the cavalry sword (i.e. a sabre). As far as correct length is concerned, there is no 'absolute'.

In British terminology, a too long or too thin tail is usually said to be '**gay**' or 'ringed'(rather like a teapot handle); it spoils the outline and the dog appears to have little control over the end of it.

In American terminology, a 'gay tail' is one that is held upwards in true hound position and carried up 'happily' - i.e. 'gaily'.

In both Standards it should be remembered that the tail is a continuation of the spine - any kinks, lumps or bumps should be carefully considered by the judge.
KC "…with a moderate amount of coarse hair underneath"; AKC "The hair on the underside of the tail is coarse."
It is not expected that any part of the tail be trimmed.

One thing not mentioned in either Standard is the fact that a white tip - or flag - is favoured by the huntsman. A Basset will indicate a 'find' with a tail stiffly held upwards and a definite wagging of the tail tip. In 'cover' or farm crops this enables the huntsman to know that the Basset has 'found' a scent.

GAIT/MOVEMENT
KC
Most important to ensure that the hound is fit for purpose. Smooth, powerful and effortless action with forelegs reaching well forward and hind legs showing powerful thrust, hound moving true both front and rear. Hocks and stifles never stiff in movement, nor must any toes be dragged.

AKC
The Basset Hound moves in a smooth, powerful, and effortless manner. Being a scenting dog with short legs, it holds its nose low to the ground. Its gait is absolutely true with perfect co-ordination between the front and hind legs, and it moves in a straight line with hind feet following in line with the front feet, the hocks well bent with no stiffness of action. The front legs do not paddle, weave, or overlap, and the elbows must lie close to the body. Going away, the hind legs are parallel.

Gait must be 'easy' fore and aft and with long strides. A Basset, despite his short legs should not mince along like a 'Regency Dandy', nor should he 'bounce' along (expending energy). The inclined forelegs (the crook) bring the forefeet in towards the centre of gravity to give a smooth action, much in the same way that a runner brings his feet towards a centre line. Therefore, there should be no plodding roll as the dog comes towards you.

One of the consequences of a short upper arm and tied-in shoulders, or elbow, is that whilst the Basset is able to stand fairly true with his feet under the body, as soon as he moves, he becomes wide in front as he strives to retain balance. The movement appears quite 'jaunty' as he attempts to remain in balance by hopping from one forefoot to the other.

'Paddling' is another incorrect movement. This is when the pasterns and feet perform a circular movement and flick outwards at each step. Again, this may be associated with a faulty shoulder construction.

'Weaving' is akin to 'paddling' and is where the forefeet cross each other's path before setting down on the ground - somewhat like the extreme walk of a couture model on the catwalk.

However, due to the shortness of the hind legs and no crook here, it is somewhat difficult for a Basset to come even close to single tracking. Therefore, a very slight roll to the hindquarters *may* be seen as the hound goes away. There should, however, be good hind extension so as to get the longest and most powerful stride.

"Elbows must lie close to the body"

MOVEMENT

The judge will assess movement from the front...

...in profile,

...and from the rear.

Flapping, loose elbows are apparent as the dog moves away but can also be found to be 'slack' during the initial examination of the hound. Conversely, 'tied-in' elbows (where the elbow is too close to the ribcage, allowing no freedom of fore movement) is also a fault.

"Hocks... never stiff in movement"
A common fault, where the hocks are permanently bent and there is no good hind extension during movement, is known as a sickle hock, after the old short-handled farming tool with a curved blade used to cut crops.
"Nor must any toes be dragged"
Where the sequence of footfall is unbalanced because of construction faults elsewhere, this often becomes apparent with the unequal wear to the toenails. It is frequently seen on the hind feet when the hindquarter angulation is not as good as the forequarter angulation.

Where the hind angulation is better than the forequarter angulation, the dog has to ensure the correct sequence of footfall is retained; otherwise, if he does not get the sequence quite right, the power from the hindquarters will cause him to trip. He will often flip up the fore feet in order to give that little extra time before the foot hits the ground. This gait is tiring and wasteful of energy. Provided the dog is equally angulated – however poorly – he will be balanced and move comfortably and with less effort, which, as far as the dog is concerned, is preferable.

COAT
KC
Smooth, short and close without being too fine. Whole outline clean and free from feathering. Long hair, soft coat or feathering highly undesirable. Skin is supple and elastic without any exaggeration.

AKC
The coat is hard, smooth, and short, with sufficient density to be of use in all weather. The skin is loose and elastic. A distinctly long coat is a disqualification.

The Basset is double coated, with a soft undercoat covered by a short, strong-haired topcoat that holds the natural body oils and should repel a certain amount of rain. (Too much bathing destroys the natural oils and the coat becomes soft and will hold the water when out in the rain.)

"Free from feathering" and *"a distinctly long coat"*
It is popularly assumed that long, soft coats were accidentally introduced to the breed by an alleged mismating between a Basset Hound and a Clumber Spaniel in Queen Alexandra's kennels in the very early 1900s. This is quite possible, but it is equally possible that, with the diverse experimental breeding taking place in the latter part of the 1800s, any long, soft-coated breed could have been introduced into a breeding programme.

"Skin is supple and elastic"
Basset types are ideal at flushing out game and, in many parts of France, the Basset Hound is still used in the forests for this purpose. Consequently, a certain looseness of skin, being supple and elastic, will 'give' as the dog hunts through brush and scrub (even briars), whereas tight-fitting skin is liable to catch and tear badly. Too much loose skin, however, is a fault that makes the hound unfit for purpose; he will hunt, but not with the same stamina because the excess skin will 'bounce' (in different directions!) thus using energy.

COLOUR
KC
Generally black, white and tan (tri-colour); lemon and white (bi-colour); but any recognised hound colour acceptable.

AKC
Any recognized hound color is acceptable and the distribution of color and markings is of no importance.

Colour and markings are immaterial. However, no part of either Standard mentions a white tip to the tail. This 'flag' is dear to the huntsman, who will be able to see where his hound is when hunting in thicket or farm crops.

Most people think of a Basset being tri-colour, with a tan head and ear leathers, upper neck (sometimes a full or part white collar here), tan flanks, upper legs and tail, a black saddle along

BASSET COLOURS

Tricolour: Black, white and tan.

Bicolour: Tan and white.

the back, and white on the muzzle, chest, lower legs and feet. Some traditional tri-colours will fade as they mature and lose most of the black.

Other tri-colours can be broken, with black tan and white in irregular patterns, often with ticking, i.e. black or brown mottling on a white background. It is likely that this goes back, in part, to the Basset Bleu de Gascogne. Sometimes a whole or part ear leather can be white, or white with black or brown ticking.

Some tri-colours will be predominantly black with tan eyebrows; they will often have tan markings at the edge of the black and then white on the feet, chest and occasionally on the foreface just above the nose. It is unusual to find a true black blanket, which has tan eyebrows and tan feet – but no white at all.

It is rare to see a true lemon and white (very pale tan and white); the bi-colours are mostly of a darker shade, described as 'red and white' (dark/mid tan and white). The lemon gene is recessive and will be masked by the more dominant red/tan gene. Markings can be wholly red (red blanket) with, perhaps, a white muzzle and/or feet or predominantly white with patches of colour and/or ticking.

A tri-colour puppy will be black and white at birth; the tan will come through later. A red and white puppy will be almost white at birth with very pale lemon/orange markings, which will darken with time. A lemon and white puppy will, at birth, be mainly white with a *very* faint pale tan marking, which will darken – but in old age this will lighten again.

SIZE
KC
Height: 33-38 cms (13-15 ins) at withers.

AKC
The height should not exceed 14 inches. Height over 15 inches at the highest point of the shoulder blade is a disqualification.

Bassets are not measured routinely. Over height is a disqualifying fault in the AKC Standard, so a measure must be called for if the judge considers the Basset to be over 15" at the withers.

FAULTS
KC
Any departure from the foregoing points should be considered a fault and the seriousness with which the fault should be regarded should be in exact proportion to its degree and its effect upon the health and welfare of the dog.

The dogs that win in the show ring will often be responsible for producing future generations.

In order to show your Basset Hound – unless dispensation has been given by the Kennel Club based on medical reasons – male animals should have two apparently normal testicles that are fully descended into the scrotum.

DISQUALIFICATIONS
AKC
Height of more than 15 inches at the highest point of the shoulder blade.
Knuckled over front legs.
Distinctly long coat.

KC
There are no disqualifications in the Standard. However, judges are expected to exclude dogs from competition if there is any *obvious* evidence of lameness, illness, infectious disease or inappropriate temperament. Judges are advised that they are able to withhold awards if they consider a dog or dogs to be of insufficient merit. If a third place is withheld, then all subsequent awards for that class must also be withheld. If a Challenge Certificate is withheld, a Best of Sex shall be awarded.

HAPPY AND HEALTHY

Chapter 8

B assets are stoical dogs with a life span that can run into double figures. The Basset is renowned as a plucky, faithful companion and a willing friend on a non-conditional basis. He will, however, of necessity rely on you for food and shelter, accident prevention and medication. A healthy Basset is a happy chap, looking to please and amuse his owner.

There are only a few genetic conditions as yet recognised in the Basset, which will be covered in depth later in the chapter.

VACCINATION
There is much debate over the issue of vaccination at the moment. The timing of the final part of the initial vaccination course for a puppy and the frequency of subsequent booster vaccinations are both under

scrutiny. An evaluation of the relative risk for each disease plays a part, depending on the local situation.

Many owners think that the actual vaccination is the protection, so that their puppy can go out for walks as soon as he or she has had the final part of the puppy vaccination course. This is not the case. The rationale behind vaccination is to stimulate the immune system into producing protective antibodies, which will be triggered if the patient is subsequently exposed to that particular disease. This means that a further one or two weeks will have to pass before an effective level of protection will have developed.

Vaccines against viruses stimulate longer-lasting protection than those against bacteria, whose effect may only persist for a matter of months in some cases.

There is also the possibility of an individual failing to mount a full immune response to a vaccination: although the vaccine schedule may have been followed as recommended, that particular dog remains vulnerable.

A dog's level of protection against rabies, as demonstrated by the antibody titre in a blood sample, used to be routinely tested in the UK in order to fulfil the requirements of the Pet Travel Scheme (PETS). From 1st January 2012, this will only apply in certain circumstances (see below). This is not required at the current time with any other individual diseases in order to gauge the need for booster vaccination or to determine the effect of a course of vaccines; instead, your veterinary surgeon will advise a protocol based upon the vaccines available, local disease prevalence, and the lifestyle of you and your dog.

It is worth remembering that maintaining a fully effective level of immune protection against the disease appropriate to your locale is vital: these are serious diseases, which may result in the death of your dog, and some may have the potential to be passed on to his human family (so-called zoonotic potential for transmission). This is where you will be grateful for your veterinary surgeon's own knowledge and advice.

The American Animal Hospital Association laid down guidance at the end of 2006 for the vaccination of dogs in North America. Core diseases were defined as distemper, adenovirus, parvovirus and rabies. So-called non-core diseases are kennel cough, Lyme disease and leptospirosis. A decision to vaccinate against one or more non-core diseases will be based on an individual's level of risk, determined on lifestyle and where you live in the US.

Do remember, however, that the booster visit to the veterinary surgery is not 'just' for a booster. I am regularly correcting my clients when they announce that they have 'just' brought their pet for a booster. Instead, this appointment is a chance for a full health check and evaluation of how a particular dog is doing. After all, we are all conversant with the adage that a human year is equivalent to seven canine years.

There have been attempts in recent times to reset the scale for two reasons: small breeds live longer than giant breeds, and dogs are living longer than previously. I have seen dogs of 17 and 18 years of age, but to say a dog is 119 or 126 years old is plainly meaningless. It does emphasise the fact, though, that a dog's health can change dramatically over the course of a single year, because dogs age at a far faster rate than humans do.

For me as a veterinary surgeon, the booster vaccination visit is a challenge: how much can I find of which the owner was unaware, such as rotten teeth or a heart murmur? Even monitoring bodyweight year upon year is of use, because bodyweight can creep up, or down, without an owner realising. Being overweight is unhealthy, but it may take an outsider's remark to make an owner realise that there is a problem. Conversely, a drop in bodyweight may be the only pointer to an underlying problem.

The diseases against which dogs are vaccinated include:

ADENOVIRUS
Canine adenovirus 1 (CAV-1) affects the liver (hepatitis) and is seen within affected dogs as the classic 'blue eye', while CAV-2 is a cause of kennel cough (see later). Vaccines often include both canine adenoviruses.

DISTEMPER
This disease is sometimes called 'hardpad' from the characteristic changes to the pads of the paws. It has a worldwide distribution, but fortunately vaccination has been very effective at reducing its occurrence. It is caused by a virus and affects the respiratory, gastro-intestinal (gut) and nervous systems, so it causes a wide range of illnesses. Fox and urban stray dog populations are most at risk and are usually responsible for local outbreaks.

KENNEL COUGH
Also known as infectious tracheobronchitis, *Bordetella*

The vet can give your dog a thorough check when you take him for his booster.

LEPTOSPIROSIS

This disease is caused by *Leptospira interrogans*, a spiral-shaped bacterium. There are several natural variants or serovars. Each is characteristically found in one or more particular host animal species, which then acts as a reservoir, intermittently shedding leptospires in the urine. Infection can also be picked up at mating, via bite wounds, across the placenta, or through eating the carcases of infected animals (such as rats).

A serovar will cause actual clinical disease in an individual when two conditions are fulfilled: the individual is not the natural host species and is also not immune to that particular serovar.

Leptospirosis is a zoonotic disease, known as Weil's disease in humans, with implications for all those in contact with an affected dog. It is also commonly called rat jaundice, reflecting the rat's important role as a carrier. The UK National Rodent Survey 2003 found a wild brown rat population of 60 million, equivalent at the time to one rat per person. Wherever you live in the UK, rats are endemic, which means that there is as much a risk to the Basset living with a family in a town as the Basset leading a rural lifestyle.

Signs of illness reflect the organs affected by a particular serovar. In humans, there may be a flu-like illness or a more serious, often life-threatening disorder involving major body organs. The illness in a susceptible dog may be mild, the dog recovering within two to three weeks without treatment but going on to develop long-term liver or kidney disease. In contrast, peracute illness may result in a rapid deterioration and death following an initial malaise and fever. There may also be anorexia, vomiting, diarrhoea, abdominal pain, joint pain, increased thirst and urination rate, jaundice, and ocular changes. Haemorrhage is also a common feature, manifesting as bleeding under the skin, nosebleeds, and the presence of blood in the urine and faeces.

Treatment requires rigorous intravenous fluid therapy to support the kidneys. Being a bacterial infection, it is possible to treat leptospirosis with specific antibiotics, although a prolonged course of several weeks is needed. Strict hygiene and barrier nursing are required in order to avoid onward transmission of the disease.

Annual vaccination is recommended for leptospirosis because the immunity only lasts for a year, unlike the longer immunity associated with vaccines against viruses. There is, however, little or no cross-protection between Leptospira serovars, so vaccination will result in protection against only those serovars included in the particular vaccine used. Additionally, although vaccination against leptospirosis will prevent active disease if an individual is exposed to a serovar included in the vaccine, it cannot prevent infection of that individual and becoming a carrier in the long-term.

In the UK, vaccines have classically included *L. icterohaemorrhagiae* (rat-adapted serovar) and *L. canicola* (dog-specific serovar). The latter is of especial significance to us humans, since disease will not be apparent in an infected dog but leptospires will be shed intermittently.

bronchiseptica is not only a major cause of kennel cough but also a common secondary infection on top of another cause. Being a bacterium, it is susceptible to treatment with appropriate antibiotics, but the immunity stimulated by the vaccine is therefore short-lived (six to 12 months).

This vaccine is often in a form to be administered down the nostrils in order to stimulate local immunity at the point of entry, so to speak. Do not be alarmed to see your veterinary surgeon using a needle and syringe to draw up the vaccine, because the needle will be replaced with a special plastic introducer, allowing the vaccine to be gently instilled into each nostril. Dogs generally resent being held more than the actual

intra-nasal vaccine, and I have learnt that covering the patient's eyes helps greatly.

Kennel cough is, however, rather a catch-all term for any cough spreading within a dog population – not just in kennels, but also between dogs at a training session or breed show, or even mixing in the park. Many of these infections may not be *B. bronchiseptica* but other viruses, for which one can only treat symptomatically. Parainfluenza virus is often included in a vaccine programme, as it is a common viral cause of kennel cough.

Kennel cough can seem alarming. There is a persistent cough accompanied by the production of white frothy spittle, which can last for a matter of

weeks; during this time the patient is highly infectious to other dogs. I remember when it ran through our five Border Collies – there were white patches of froth on the floor wherever you looked! Other features include sneezing, a runny nose, and eyes sore with conjunctivitis. Fortunately, these infections are generally self-limiting, most dogs recovering without any long-lasting problems, but an elderly dog may be knocked sideways by it, akin to the effects of a common cold on a frail, elderly person.

LYME DISEASE
This is a bacterial infection transmitted by hard ticks. It is restricted to those specific areas of the US where ticks are found, such as the north-eastern states,

Kennel Cough is highly infectious and will spread rapidly among dogs that live together.

RABIES

This is another zoonotic disease and there are very strict control measures in place. Vaccines were once available in the UK only on an individual basis for dogs being taken abroad. Pets travelling into the UK had to serve six months' compulsory quarantine so that any pet incubating rabies would be identified before release back into the general population. Under the UK Pet Travel Scheme (PETS), provided certain criteria are met (check the DEFRA website for up-to-date information – www.defra.gov.uk) dogs can enter the UK without being quarantined. From 1st January 2012, a dog living in EU and specified non-EU countries such as the USA can travel 21 days after being microchipped and vaccinated against rabies. The requirement for a blood test thirty days after rabies vaccination, with a result demonstrating effective immunity, still applies to dogs from certain non-EU countries such as South Africa, together with a three month wait from the date of that blood test before being allowed to enter the UK.

Dogs to be imported into the US have to show that they were vaccinated against rabies at least 30 days previously; otherwise, they have to serve effective internal quarantine for 30 days from the date of vaccination against rabies, in order to ensure they are not incubating rabies. The exception is dogs entering from countries recognised as being rabies-free, in which case it has to be proved that they lived in that country for at least six months beforehand. Regulations do change so ensure you have up-to-date information.

some southern states, California and the upper Mississippi region. It does also occur in the UK, but at a low level, so vaccination is not routinely offered.

Clinical disease is manifested primarily as limping due to arthritis, but other organs affected include the heart, kidneys and nervous system. It is readily treatable with appropriate antibiotics, once diagnosed, but the causal bacterium, *Borrelia burgdorferi*, is not cleared from the body totally and will persist.

Prevention requires both vaccination and tick control, especially as there are other diseases transmitted by ticks. Ticks carrying *B. burgdorferi* will transmit it to humans as well, but an infected dog cannot pass it to a human.

PARVOVIRUS (CPV)

Canine parvovirus disease first appeared in the late 1970s, when it was feared that the UK's dog population would be decimated by it because of the lack of immunity in the general canine population. While this was a terrifying possibility at the time, fortunately it did not happen.

There are two forms of the virus (CPV-1, CPV-2) affecting domesticated dogs. It is highly contagious, picked up via the mouth/nose from infected faeces. The incubation period is about five days. CPV-2 causes two types of illness: gastro-enteritis and heart disease in puppies born to unvaccinated dams, both of which often result in death. Infection of puppies under three weeks of age with CPV-1 manifests as diarrhoea, vomiting, difficulty breathing, and fading puppy syndrome. CPV-1 can cause abortion and foetal abnormalities in breeding bitches.

Occurrence is mainly low now, thanks to vaccination, although a

The breeder will have started a worming programme which you will need to continue.

recent outbreak in my area did claim the lives of several dogs. It is also occasionally seen in the elderly unvaccinated dog.

PARASITES
A parasite is defined as an organism deriving benefit on a one-way basis from another, the host. It goes without saying that it is not to the parasite's advantage to harm the host to such an extent that the benefit is lost, especially if it results in the death of the host. This means a dog could harbour parasites, internal and/or external, without there being any signs apparent to the owner. Many canine parasites can, however, transfer to humans with variable consequences, so routine preventative treatment is advised against particular parasites.

Just as with vaccination, risk assessment plays a part – for example, there is no need for routine heartworm treatment in the UK (at present), but it is vital in the US and in Mediterranean countries.

ROUNDWORMS (NEMATODES)
These are the spaghetti-like worms that you may have seen passed in faeces or brought up in vomit. Most of the deworming treatments in use today cause the adult roundworms to disintegrate, thankfully, so that treating puppies in particular is not as unpleasant as it used to be!

Most puppies will have a worm burden, mainly of a particular roundworm species (*Toxocara canis*), which reactivates within the dam's tissues during pregnancy and passes to the foetuses developing in the womb. It is therefore important to treat the dam both during and after pregnancy, as well as the puppies.

Professional advice is to continue worming every one to three months. There are roundworm eggs in the environment and, unless you examine your dog's faeces under a microscope on a very regular basis for the presence of roundworm eggs, you will be unaware of your dog having picked up roundworms, unless he should have such a heavy burden that he passes the adults.

It takes a few weeks from the time that a dog swallows a *Toxocara canis* roundworm egg to himself passing viable eggs (the pre-patent period). These eggs are not immediately infective to other animals, requiring a period of maturation in the environment, which is primarily temperature-dependent and therefore shorter in the summer (as little as two weeks) than in the winter. The eggs can survive in the environment for two years and more.

There are deworming products that are active all the time, which will provide continuous protection when administered as often as directed. Otherwise, treating every month will, in effect, cut in before a dog could theoretically become a source of roundworm eggs to the general population.

It is the risk to human health that is so important: *T. canis* roundworms will migrate within our tissues and cause all manner of problems, not least of which (but fortunately rarely) is blindness. If a dog has roundworms, the eggs also find their way on to his coat where they can be picked up during stroking. Sensible hygiene is therefore important. You should always carefully pick up your

HEARTWORM

Heartworm infection has been diagnosed in dogs all over the world. There are two prerequisites: the presence of mosquitoes, and a warm, humid climate.

When a female mosquito bites an infected animal, it acquires D. immitis in its circulating form, as microfilariae. A warm environmental temperature is needed for these microfilariae to develop into the infective third-stage larvae (L3) within the mosquitoes, the so-called intermediate host. L3 larvae are then transmitted by the mosquito when it next bites a dog. Therefore, while heartworm infection is found in all parts of the United States, it is at differing levels. An occurrence in Alaska, for example, is probably a reflection of a visiting dog having previously picked up the infection elsewhere.

Heartworm infection is not currently a problem in the UK. Most infected dogs in the UK contract it while abroad because they have not had suitable preventative treatment. However, there have been a small number of cases in dogs that have not left the country. Global warming and its effect on the UK's climate could change things significantly in the future.

It is a potentially life-threatening condition, with dogs of all breeds and ages being susceptible without preventative treatment. The larvae can grow to 14 inches within the right side of the heart, causing primarily signs of heart failure and ultimately liver and kidney damage. It can be treated but prevention is a better plan. In the US, regular blood tests for the presence of infection are advised, coupled with appropriate preventative measures, so I would advise liaison with your veterinary surgeon.

For dogs travelling to heartworm-endemic areas of the EU, such as the Mediterranean coast, preventative treatment should be started before leaving the UK and maintained during the visit. Again, this is best arranged with your veterinary surgeon.

dog's faeces and dispose of them appropriately, thereby preventing the maturation of any eggs present in the fresh faeces.

TAPEWORMS (CESTODES)
When considering the general dog population, the primary source of the commonest tapeworm species will be fleas, which can carry the eggs. Most multi-wormers will be active against these tapeworms. They are not a threat to human health, but it is unpleasant to see the wriggly ricegrain tapeworm segments emerging from your dog's back passage while he is lying in front of the fire, and usually when you have guests for dinner!

A tapeworm of significance to human health is *Echinococcus granulosus*, found in a few parts of the UK, mainly in Wales. Man is an intermediate host for this

tapeworm, along with sheep, cattle and pigs. Inadvertent ingestion of eggs passed in the faeces of an infected dog is followed by the development of so-called hydatid cysts in major organs, such as the lungs and liver, necessitating surgical removal. Dogs become infected through eating raw meat containing hydatid cysts. Cooking will kill hydatid cysts, so avoid feeding raw meat and offal in areas of high risk.

The specific requirements for treatment with praziquantel within 24 to 48 hours of entry into the UK under the Pet Travel Scheme are under review. They were put in place to prevent the inadvertent introduction of *Echinococcus multilocularis*, a tapeworm carried by foxes on mainland Europe, which is transmissible to humans, causing serious or even fatal liver

disease. You should therefore still consider precautionary treatment of your dog.

FLEAS
There are several species of flea, which are not host-specific. A dog can be carrying cat and human fleas as well as dog fleas, but the same flea treatment will kill and/or control them all. It is also accepted that environmental control is a vital part of a flea control programme. This is because the adult flea is only on the animal for as long as it takes to have a blood meal and to breed; the remainder of the life cycle occurs in the house, car, caravan, shed...

There is a vast array of flea control products available, with various routes of administration: collar, powder, spray, 'spot-on', or oral. Flea control needs to be applied to all pets in the house, regardless of whether they leave the house, since fleas can be introduced into the home by other pets and their human owners. Discuss your specific flea control needs with your veterinary surgeon.

MITES
There are five types of mite that can affect dogs.

Demodex canis: This mite is a normal inhabitant of canine hair follicles, passed from the bitch to her pups as they suckle. The development of actual skin disease or demodicosis depends on the individual. It is seen frequently around the time of

Investigation is required if your Basset is continually scratching,

puberty and after a bitch's first season, associated with hormonal changes. There may, however, be an inherited weakness in an individual's immune system, enabling multiplication of the mite.

The localised form consists of areas of fur loss without itchiness, generally around the face and on the forelimbs, and 90 per cent will recover without treatment. The other 10 per cent develop the juvenile-onset generalised form, of which half will recover spontaneously. The other half may be depressed, go off their food, and show signs of itchiness due to secondary bacterial skin infections.

Treatment is often prolonged over several months and consists of regular bathing with a specific miticidal shampoo, often clipping away fur to improve access to the skin, together with a suitable antibiotic by mouth. There is also now a licensed 'spot-on' preparation available. Progress is monitored by the examination of deep skin scrapings for the presence of the mite; the initial diagnosis is based upon abnormally high numbers of the mite, often with live individuals being seen.

Some Bassets may develop demodicosis for the first time in middle-age (more than four years of age). This often reflects underlying immunosuppression by an internal disease, so it is important to identify such a cause and correct it where possible, as well as treating the skin condition.

Sarcoptes scabei: This characteristically causes an intense pruritus or itchiness in the affected Basset, causing him to

TICKS

Ticks have become an increasing problem in recent years throughout Britain. Their physical presence causes irritation, but it is their potential to spread disease that causes concern. A tick will transmit any infection previously contracted while feeding on an animal: for example Borrelia burgdorferi, the causal agent of Lyme disease (see page 132).

The life cycle of the tick is curious: each life stage takes a year to develop and move on to the next. Long grass is a major habitat. The vibration of animals moving through the grass will stimulate the larva, nymph or adult to climb up a blade of grass and wave its legs in the air as it 'quests' for a host on to which to latch for its next blood meal. Humans are as likely to be hosts, so ramblers and orienteers are advised to cover their legs when going through rough long grass.

There are effective treatments against ticks. Removing a tick is simple – provided your dog will stay still. The important rule is to twist gently so that the tick is persuaded to let go with its mouthparts. Grasp the body of the tick as near to your dog's skin as possible, either between thumb and fingers or with a specific tick-removing instrument, and then rotate in one direction until the tick comes away. I keep a plastic tick hook in my wallet at all times.

Ticks elsewhere in the world are an important vector of diseases. There was a requirement under the UK Pet Travel Scheme for tick treatment within 24-48 hours of a dog entering the UK. From 1st January 2012, this is no longer the case. You should, however, take action to protect your dog from picking up ticks if travelling abroad in a high risk area.

incessantly scratch and bite at himself, leading to marked fur loss and skin trauma. Initially starting on the elbows, earflaps and hocks, without treatment the skin on the rest of the body can become affected, with thickening and pigmentation of the skin. Secondary bacterial infections are common.

Unlike Demodex, this mite lives at the skin surface, and it can be hard to find in skin scrapings. It is therefore not unusual to treat a patient for sarcoptic mange (scabies) based on the appearance of the problem even with negative skin scraping findings, and especially if there is a history of contact with foxes, which are a frequent source of the scabies mite.

It will spread between dogs and can therefore also be found in situations where large numbers of dogs from different backgrounds mix together. It will cause itchiness in humans, although the mite cannot complete its life cycle on us, so treating all affected dogs should be sufficient. Fortunately, there are now highly effective 'spot-on' treatments for Sarcoptes scabei.

Cheyletiella yasguri: This is the fur mite most commonly found on dogs. It is often called 'walking dandruff' because it can be possible to see collections of the small white mite moving about over the skin surface. There is excessive scale and dandruff formation, and mild itchiness. It

is transmissible to humans, causing a pruritic rash.

Diagnosis is by microscopic examination of skin scrapings, coat combings and sticky tape impressions from the skin and fur. Treatment is with an appropriate insecticide, as advised by your veterinary surgeon.

Otodectes cynotis: A highly transmissible otitis externa (outer ear infection) results from the presence in the outer ear canal of this ear mite, characterised by exuberant production of dark earwax. The patient will frequently shake his head and rub at the ear(s) affected. The mites can also spread on to the skin adjacent to the opening of the external ear canal, and may transfer elsewhere,

EAR INFECTIONS

The dog has a long external ear canal, initially vertical then horizontal, leading to the eardrum, which protects the middle ear. If your Basset is shaking his head, then his ears will need to be inspected with an auroscope by a veterinary surgeon in order to identify any cause and to ensure the eardrum is intact. A sample may be taken from the canal to be examined under the microscope and cultured, to identify causal agents before prescribing appropriate eardrops containing antibiotic, antifungal agent and/or steroid. Predisposing causes of otitis externa or

infection in the external ear canal include:
• Presence of a foreign body, such as a grass awn
• Ear mites, which are intensely irritating to the dog and stimulate the production of brown wax, predisposing to infection
• Previous infections, causing the canal's lining to thicken, narrowing the canal and reducing ventilation
• Bathing/swimming – water trapped in the external ear canal can lead to infection, especially if the water is not clean.

such as to the paws.

When using an otoscope to examine the outer ear canal, the heat from the light source will often cause any ear mites present to start moving around. I often offer owners the chance to have a look, because it really is quite an extraordinary sight! It is also possible to identify the mite from earwax smeared on to a slide and examined under a microscope.

Cats are a common source of ear mites. It is not unusual to find ear mites during the routine examination of puppies and kittens. Treatment options include specific eardrops acting against both the mite and any secondary infections present in the auditory canal, and certain 'spot-on' formulations. It is vital to treat all dogs and cats in the household to prevent recycling of the mite between individuals.

(Neo-) Trombicula autumnalis:

The free-living harvest mite can cause an intense local irritation on the skin. Its larvae are picked up from undergrowth, so they are characteristically found as a bright orange patch on the web of skin between the digits of the paws. It feeds on skin cells before dropping off to complete its life cycle in the environment.

Its name is a little misleading, because it is not restricted to the autumn nor to harvest-time; I find it on the earflaps of cats from late June onwards, depending on the prevailing weather. It will also bite humans.

Treatment depends on identifying and avoiding hotspots

A responsible owner will be aware of some of the health problems that can affect Bassets.

for picking up harvest mites, if possible. Checking the skin, especially the paws, after exercise and mechanically removing any mites found will reduce the chances of irritation, which can be treated symptomatically. Insecticides can also be applied be guided by your veterinary surgeon.

A-Z OF AILMENTS

ANAL SACS (IMPACTED)

The anal sacs lie on either side of the anus at approximately four and eight o'clock, if compared with the face of a clock. They fill with a particularly pungent fluid, which is emptied on to the faeces as they move past the sacs to exit from the anus. Theories abound as to why these sacs should

become impacted periodically and seemingly more so in some dogs than others.

The irritation of impacted anal sacs is often seen as 'scooting', when the backside is dragged along the ground. Some dogs will also gnaw at their back feet or over the rump.

Increasing the fibre content of the diet helps some dogs; in others, there is underlying skin disease. It may be a one-off occurrence for no apparent reason. Sometimes an infection can become established, requiring antibiotic therapy, which may need to be coupled with flushing out the infected sac under sedation or general anaesthesia. More rarely, a dog will present with an apparently acute-onset anal sac abscess, which is incredibly painful.

DIARRHOEA
Cause and treatment much as Gastritis (see below).

FOREIGN BODIES
- **Internal:** Items swallowed in haste without checking whether they will be digested can cause problems if they lodge in the stomach or obstruct the intestines, necessitating surgical removal. Acute vomiting is the main indication. Common objects I have seen removed include stones from the garden, peach stones, babies' dummies, golf balls, and, once, a lady's bra... It is possible to diagnose a dog with an intestinal obstruction across a waiting room from a particularly 'tucked-up' stance and pained facial expression. These patients bounce back from surgery dramatically. A previously docile and compliant obstructed patient will return for a post-operative check-up and literally bounce into the consulting room.

- **External:** Grass awns are adept at finding their way into orifices such as a nostril, down an ear, and into the soft skin between two digits (toes), whence they start a one-way journey due to the direction of their whiskers. In particular, I remember a grass awn that migrated from a hindpaw, causing abscesses along the way but not yielding itself up until it erupted through the skin in the groin!

GASTRITIS
This is usually a simple stomach upset, most commonly in response to dietary indiscretion. Scavenging constitutes a change in the diet as much as an abrupt switch in the food being fed by the owner.

There are also some specific infections causing more severe gastritis/enteritis, which will require treatment from a veterinary surgeon (see also Canine Parvovirus under 'Vaccination' on page 127).

Generally, a day without food, followed by a few days of small, frequent meals of a bland diet (such as cooked chicken or fish), or an appropriate prescription diet, should allow the stomach to settle. It is vital to ensure the patient is drinking and retaining sufficient water to cover losses resulting from the stomach upset in addition to the normal losses to be expected when healthy. Oral rehydration fluid may not be very appetising for the patient, in which case cooled boiled water should be offered. Fluids should initially be

GROWTH-PLATE DAMAGE

This can result from an inadvertent lack of attention by new owners to their puppy's activities - for example, when the puppy has been over-exercised (especially on hard surfaces), allowed to go up and down steps, and/or permitted to jump on and off furniture. It can, however, be hard to curtail an exuberant puppy.

In the legs, the 'growth plate' is situated at each end of the long bones. The front legs are most commonly affected at the dog's 'wrist' or carpus. The plate is very often damaged on the outer side of the leg. This damage stops the growth plate from developing and causes the foot to turn outwards, resulting in 'Queen Anne' legs. Later in life this damage can lead to arthritic problems in the forequarters. It can take as long as 12 months for some growth plates to mature.

offered in small but frequent amounts to avoid over-drinking, which can result in further vomiting and thereby dehydration and electrolyte imbalances. It is also important to wean the patient back on to routine food gradually or else another bout of gastritis may occur.

JOINT PROBLEMS

It is not unusual for older Bassets to be stiff after exercise, particularly in cold weather. This is not really surprising, given that they can be quite busy dogs when young. The Basset is a game breed: a nine- or ten-year-old Basset will not readily forego an extra walk or take kindly to turning for home earlier than usual. Your veterinary surgeon will be able to advise you on ways of helping your dog cope with stiffness, not least of which will be to ensure that he is not overweight. Arthritic joints do not need to be burdened with extra bodyweight!

LUMPS

Regularly handling and stroking your dog will enable the early detection of lumps and bumps. These may be due to infection (abscess), bruising, multiplication of particular cells from within the body, or even an external parasite (tick). If you are worried about any lump you find, have it checked by a veterinary surgeon.

OBESITY

Being overweight does predispose to many other problems, such as diabetes mellitus, heart disease

and joint problems. It is so easily prevented by simply acting as your Basset's conscience. Ignore pleading eyes and feed according to your dog's waistline. The body condition is what matters qualitatively, alongside monitoring that individual's bodyweight as a quantitative measure. The Basset should, in my opinion as a health professional, have at least a suggestion of a waist and it should be possible to feel the ribs beneath only a slight layer of fat.

Neutering does not automatically mean that your Basset will be overweight. Having an ovario-hysterectomy does slow down the body's rate of working, castration to a lesser extent, but it therefore means that your dog needs less food. I recommend cutting back a little on the amount of food fed a few weeks before neutering to accustom your Basset to less food. If she looks a little underweight on the morning of the operation, it will help the veterinary surgeon as well as giving her a little leeway weight-wise afterwards. It is always harder to lose weight after neutering than before, because of this slowing in the body's inherent metabolic rate.

TEETH PROBLEMS

Eating food starts with the canine teeth gripping and killing prey in the wild, incisor teeth biting off pieces of food and the molar teeth chewing it. To be able to eat is vital for life, yet the actual health of the teeth is often overlooked: unhealthy teeth can predispose to disease, and not just by reducing the ability to eat. The presence of infection within the mouth can lead to bacteria entering the bloodstream and then filtering out at major organs, with the potential for

A fit, active Basset will live a longer, healthier life.

serious consequences. That is not to forget that simply having dental pain can affect a dog's wellbeing, as anyone who has had toothache will confirm.

Veterinary dentistry has made huge leaps in recent years, so that it no longer consists of extraction as the treatment of necessity. Good dental health lies in the hands of the owner, starting from the moment the dog comes into your care. Just as we have taken on responsibility for feeding, so we have acquired the task of maintaining good dental and oral hygiene. In an ideal world, we should brush our dogs' teeth as regularly as our own, but the Basset puppy who finds having his teeth brushed is a huge game and excuse to roll over and over on the ground requires loads of patience, twice a day.

There are alternative strategies, ranging from dental chewsticks to specially formulated foods, but the main thing is to be aware of your dog's mouth. At least train your puppy to permit full examination of his teeth. This will not only ensure you are checking in his mouth regularly but will also make your veterinary surgeon's job easier when there is a real need for your dog to 'open wide!'

INHERITED AND PREDISPOSED DISORDERS

Any individual, dog or human, may have an inherited disorder by virtue of the genes acquired from the parents. This is significant not only for the health of that individual but also because of the potential for transmitting the disorder on to that individual's offspring and to subsequent generations, depending on the mode of inheritance.

There are control schemes in place for some inherited disorders. In the US, for example, the Canine Eye Registration Foundation (CERF) was set up by dog breeders concerned about heritable eye disease, and provides a database of dogs who have been examined by diplomates of the American College of Veterinary Ophthalmologists.

Your new puppy has been carefully bred and appears to be

All breeding stock should be subject to health clearances.

BLOAT (GASTRIC DILATATION/VOLVULUS OR GDV)

Basset Hounds do have a tendency to suffer from bloat, and it can lead to premature death. Bloat occurs when there is excessive accumulation of gas within the stomach, which becomes distended (gastric dilatation) and may twist (GDV). Complications arise if the stomach twists to such an extent that it cannot empty so it continues to fill with gas, and the spleen may also become involved. Without prompt attention, all manner of complications can develop, which may, ultimately, prove fatal. Time is of the essence with this condition.

It is therefore important for you to be aware of the signs of GDV so that its development can be spotted at as early a stage as possible. These include:
- Non-productive retching
- Failing to settle, repeatedly standing and stretching
- Anxiety and flank-gazing
- Excessive salivation.

The abdomen may not actually look bloated in the initial stages. Depression and collapse occur in the later stages.

Early aggressive treatment is vital. Radiography will help distinguish between simple bloat requiring treatment for shock and decompression of the stomach in the first instance, and GDV that is a far more serious situation. Treatment of GDV requires surgical attention despite the increased anaesthetic risks posed. The stomach may be anchored in place at this point, or as a separate surgical procedure after recovery when the patient is a better risk for surgery. Monitoring of heart function and changes in the blood are continued through to the post-operative period.

Anchoring the stomach in place greatly reduces the chances of volvulus, but does not prevent simple bloat. It may be carried out at the same time as a routine surgery, such as spaying, if an individual is felt to be at high risk. Much work has been carried out to identify risk factors with some conflicting results, not least because the actual cause of GDV is unclear. For example, feeding from a height is often advised as a preventive measure, yet other research has found that this increases the risk of GDV developing. Other risk factors include:
- Being related to an individual who has experienced GDV
- Feeding once daily rather than offering smaller meals during the day
- Feeding dried food
- Exercise after eating a meal
- Previous occurrence of GDV.

There is no doubt that the key to surviving GDV is early intervention, much like the situation with colic in the horse. Contact your veterinary surgeon if you are at all concerned that your Basset may be showing signs of GDV. On no account go to bed hoping the dog will improve by morning – he will not survive the night.

BASSET HOUND THROMBOPATHIA

This is an inherited blood-clotting disorder arising from faulty platelet aggregation. There is a spectrum of effects, ranging from a tendency to bruising to severe haemorrhage. It usually becomes apparent at a young age as unexpected bleeding, such as a nose bleed, the appearance of bruises or small haemorrhages (in the skin, ears or mouth, for example), or prolonged bleeding after an apparently minor wound. It may not, however, manifest until routine surgery is first performed, such as neutering.

in good health. The puppy shows no sign of the following, and, apart from the possibility of skin problems, is unlikely to do so throughout its life. None of the problems is specific to Bassets but they have been known to occur within the breed.

ELBOW DYSPLASIA

A form of elbow dysplasia (ununited anconeal process) occurs in the Basset Hound. The *BVA/KC Elbow Dysplasia Scheme screens for this inherited condition by assessing a radiograph taken of each elbow after the age of one year.

EYELID DEFORMITIES

There is a breed predisposition to entropion and ectropion (respectively the rolling in and out of an eyelid), and the combined entropion-ectropion of so-called diamond eye. Whilst ectropion may be simply a cosmetic feature, entropion may need surgical correction to alleviate the discomfort and pain of the inturned eyelid rubbing against the outer surface of the eye.

GLAUCOMA, ANGLE-CLOSURE OR PRIMARY

Evidence indicates the incidence of predisposition may be quite high, but the incidence of the disease itself remains extremely low. Consequently, occurrence of a fluid pressure build-up inside the eye is very rare. If pressure build-up does happen, the dog can be in considerable pain and it can be mistaken for ear or intervertebral disc problems. Early diagnosis and treatment are of the essence to prevent damage to the optic nerve.

Clinical signs can appear at any age but usually in middle age. Assessment by gonioscopy can enable a predisposition to angle closure glaucoma to be identified as early as four months of age. It is controlled under Schedule A of the **BVA/KC/ISDS Scheme in the UK, CERF in the US.

* British Veterinary Association/Kennel Club
** British Veterinary Association/Kennel Club/International Sheepdog Society Scheme

INTERVERTEBRAL DISC DISEASE (IVDD)

The Basset's characteristically short, thick limbs result from abnormal development of the cartilage. This can, however, also affect the intervertebral discs, which lie between the bodies of the vertebrae of the bony spine to act as shock absorbers. The normal intervertebral disc consists of an annulus fibrosus, which surrounds and contains the jellylike nucleus; in breeds such as the Basset, the annulus fibrosus becomes more like cartilage, so that it is less able to contain the nucleus and prevent it from herniating into the spinal canal.

IVDD first occurs in the young mature Basset of three to six or seven years of age. One or more intervertebral discs may be affected. There is a sudden onset of pain; other effects - such as weakness, inco-ordination, lameness or paralysis, sensation defects and loss of control over bladder and bowels - are variable, depending on the area of the spinal cord affected and the degree of compression. Diagnosis is often initially presumptive, based on the sudden onset of these clinical signs in a young Basset.

A full neurological appraisal of the patient will help towards identifying the area or areas of the vertebral column affected. Plain radiographs reveal bony abnormalities and mineralisation of intervertebral discs. Contrast radiography or myelography reveals where spinal cord compression is occurring, and will yield a sample of cerebro-spinal fluid, which can be analysed to rule out other causes. Myelography has been superseded by MRI at centres with a scanner, which has the advantage of being a non-invasive procedure.

Left untreated, there is the real possibility of permanent paralysis and incontinence. There can be a good response to pain relief and cage rest, but surgical treatment to relieve the pressure on the spinal cord is often required and especially after repeat episodes. Surgery may not always be successful, determined by factors such as the time between onset of clinical signs and surgery, the nature and severity of the effects of spinal cord compression and the presence or absence of deep pain sensation.

Maintaining your Basset at an ideal body condition and fitness is important, as well as avoiding jumping and twisting movements if possible.

PANOSTEITIS

Panosteitis is also known as enostosis, 'Dutch limp' or simply 'growing pains'. This is prevalent in certain lines. It is a disease characterised by the production of scar tissue in the interior of bone and the production of new bone within the marrow cavity, resulting in a characteristic radiological appearance. The ulna, humerus, radius, tibia and fibula are the bones that are usually affected. The causes are thought to be multifactorial and may include viral origin, genetic predisposition and over-nutrition.

The disease is often episodic and is most frequently identified in Bassets aged six to ten months. Some rare cases have been reported in older animals. An acute onset of lameness is frequently the first sign of panosteitis, commonly affecting a forelimb, less often a hindlimb. The lameness may seem to 'shift' from limb to limb. The dog may also suffer from other symptoms associated with pain, including inappetence, a high temperature and apathy.

The unique conformation of the Basset Hound can lead to disc problems.

Visual clinical signs may persist for several months but - with appropriate rest, therapy and good dietary management - it has usually resolved by the time skeletal development is complete. It is not unusual, however, for there to be concurrent elbow dysplasia complicating the clinical picture, for example, since they manifest at similar ages. Radiography is therefore vital for a full diagnosis to be made.

PERSISTENT MULLERIAN DUCT SYNDROME (PMDS)

This is a very rare form of pseudo-hermaphroditism, resulting in a male Basset with oviducts, uterus and cranial vagina. This has been diagnosed in Bassets in Europe and the Antipodes.

Clinical signs of PMDS are indicative of lower urinary tract disease, and can be similar to a womb infection (pyometra) in the bitch, including abdominal pain and passage of urine containing blood. Research is being undertaken in Holland and Paris (Glasgow and Cambridge Veterinary Schools are taking an interest in Britain). Surgery can be performed to correct this anomaly.

WOBBLER SYNDROME (CERVICAL VERTEBRAL MALFORMATION/MALARTICULATION, CERVICAL SPONDYLOPATHY)

This is not common and is unlikely to manifest in a dog older than 12 months. Abnormalities in the shape and articulation of vertebral bones in the neck region result in the spinal cord being pinched as it runs through the spinal canal. This affects the dog's co-ordination, particularly in the hind movement. An affected Basset may show only mild signs (slightly wandery or wobbly gait, standing with limbs wider apart than would be expected, scuffed hind-claws, for example) or, at the other extreme, be unable to walk at all. Most vets are familiar with this condition but may refer the dog to a specialist.

COMPLEMENTARY THERAPIES

Just as for human health, I do believe that there is a place for alternative therapies alongside and complementing orthodox treatment under the supervision of a veterinary surgeon. That is why 'complementary therapies' is a better name.

Because animals do not have a choice, there are measures in place to safeguard their wellbeing and welfare. All manipulative treatment must be under the direction of a veterinary surgeon who has examined the patient and diagnosed the condition that he or she feels needs that form of treatment. This covers physiotherapy, chiropractic, osteopathy and swimming therapy. For example, dogs with arthritis who cannot exercise as freely as they were accustomed will enjoy the sensation of

SKIN PROBLEMS

The Basset is prone to several skin conditions. It is important to keep your Basset in clean, dry conditions and not on damp concrete. Particular attention must be paid to keeping the folds in the skin dry after a walk.

Pododermatitis is a skin infection affecting the paws, most often the forepaws.

Malassezia or yeast infections of the skin are common, often showing a seasonal pattern of occurrence.

Primary seborrhoea becomes apparent in the young Basset as a greasy, scurfy coat and predisposes to skin infections.

Your veterinary surgeon may suggest feeding an exclusion diet in order to identify any underlying food hypersensitivity complicating your Basset's skin condition.

Complementary therapies can be of real benefit when used in conjunction with conventional medicine.

controlled non-weight-bearing exercise in water, and will benefit with improved muscling and overall fitness.

All other complementary therapies, such as acupuncture, homoeopathy and aromatherapy, can only be carried out by veterinary surgeons who have been trained in that particular field. Acupuncture is mainly used in dogs for pain relief, often to good effect. The needles look more alarming to the owner, but they are very fine and are well tolerated by most canine patients. Speaking personally, superficial needling is not unpleasant and does help with pain relief.

Homoeopathy has had a mixed press in recent years. It is based on the concept of treating like with like. Additionally, a homoeopathic remedy is said to become more powerful the more it is diluted.

SUMMARY

As the owner of a Basset, you are responsible for his care and health. Not only must you make decisions on his behalf, you are also responsible for establishing a lifestyle for him that will ensure he leads a long and happy life. Diet plays an important a part in this, as does exercise.

For the domestic dog, it is only in recent years that the need has been recognised for changing the diet to suit the dog as he grows, matures and then enters his twilight years. So-called life-stage diets try to match the nutritional needs of the dog as he progresses through life.

An adult dog food will suit the Basset living a standard family life. There are also foods for those Bassets tactfully termed as obese-prone, such as those who have been neutered or are less active than others, or simply like

their food. Do remember, though, that ultimately you are in control of your Basset's diet, unless he is able to profit from scavenging!

On the other hand, prescription diets are of necessity fed under the supervision of a veterinary surgeon because each is formulated to meet the very specific needs of particular health conditions. Should a prescription diet be fed to a healthy dog, or to a dog with a different illness, there could be adverse effects.

It is important to remember that your Basset has no choice. As his owner, you are responsible for any decision made, so it must be as informed a decision as possible. Always speak to your vet if you have any worries about your Basset. He is not just a dog; from the moment you brought him home, he became a member of the family.

THE CONTRIBUTORS

THE EDITORS:
COLIN & TRISH WELLS (KORTEBIN)

Colin and Trish Wells purchased their first Basset Hound in 1970 and their Kortebin 'line' is descended from this bitch. Colin is the Treasurer and Trish is the Vice-Chairman of the Midland Basset Hound Club. Both serve on a number of other Canine Society Committees and have also helped to run a very popular Ringcraft training group. Colin served as the Kennel Club Shows Liaison Officer for the North East for a number of years.

Trish is a graduate of the Canine Studies Judging Diploma and both Colin and Trish have been passed, by the Kennel Club, to award Challenge Certificates in Basset Hounds. Colin has also been passed to award CC's in Bassets Fauve de Bretagne and Trish in five other hound breeds. They have both judged in other parts of the World. Both Colin and Trish appear on the judging lists of a number of breeds from all 7 Groups and both have judged Best In Show, at Open Show level, on a number of occasions.

Trish writes the weekly Basset Hound Breed Notes and also an occasional column on varying canine subjects for the *Our Dogs* newspaper.

See Chapter One: Getting To Know Basset Hounds; Chapter Two: The First Basset Hounds; Chapter Three: A Basset For Your Lifestyle; Chapter Four: The New Arrival; Chapter Five: The Best of Care; Chapter Seven: The Perfect Basset Hound.

TINA WATKINS (BLACKVEIN)

Tina Watkins joined the Basset Hound Club of Wales in 1992 and currently serves as Treasurer (an office she has held since 1993), and assistant Secretary as well as being heavily involved with the preparation work for the BHC of Wales Seminars. Tina Shows and breeds her Bassets under the Blackvein affix and is a Kennel Club Accredited Breeder. She has been passed by the Kennel Club to award Challenge Certificates. Tina is well known around her surrounding area and is the Chairman of a local canine society where she is always happy to help and share her knowledge.

See Chapter One: "Bassets As Therapy Dogs", "Joining A Breed Club", "Helping Others"; Chapter Three: "Introduction", "Finding A Basset Puppy".

CATH WHITEHEAD (ARDENMILL)

Cath Whitehead obtained her first two Basset Hounds in 1987 – two brothers from Mrs Dynes. Cath says, "I wanted a Dachshund and my husband wanted a Bloodhound, so we plumped for Bassets instead. I was against it, because we were both out at work all day, so we only went to look – but we came back with two puppies. We did everything wrong, we had two puppies no equipment and only the food (about a week's worth from the breeder). We dashed home in the car with the puppies in the foot well on paper which was good because they both messed in the car (the smell was terrible). We arrived at the pet shop to buy beds, bedding, bowls, leads etc. then home for the puppies to have a bath and the car to have a clean.

"Mrs Dynes booked us and the puppies into the Ladies Kennel Association (LKA) show. Andyne the Welsh Dragon took first in the puppy class which qualified him for Crufts – which we attended and he took first there as well. We were 'hooked'.

"During that time I became interested in judging and started attending seminars on the breed (I obtained a Pass and also obtained the first assessment toward the requirement for the A2 judging list). I enrolled on the Canine Studies Judging Diploma, which was a correspondence course. The course was supposed to take six months but took nearly 12. It was very hard to keep up with the course work, hold down a full-time job, walk and care for my dogs, show them, look after the house, etc. I used to get up with my husband at 3am (as he was a lorry driver then) and start typing up my homework while it was quiet and there were no distractions. I passed - which was wonderful.

"I am secretary of the Midland Basset Hound Club and am now passed by the Kennel Club to award Challenge Certificates in the Breed."

See Chapter One: "Working With Bassets".

ROB COULBERT (HOUNDSTONE)

Rob Coulbert 'married' into Basset Hounds. His wife, Pam, shows her Bassets under the Houndstone kennel name, Pam is passed by the Kennel Club to award Challenge Certificates. Rob is a part-time Construction Engineer and part-time Deer Stalker (as seen on British television's 'Country Lives'). As a Gun Club Member, Rob enjoys making Vintage Rifles outscore the modern, expensive, ones.

As much as going out with Rob and his gun, Houndstone Madelaine May also enjoys dog shows with Pam and has gained two Challenge Certificates.

See Chapter Two: "Houndstone Madelaine May".

PETER GUY (RAGGALDS)

Peter Guy and his wife Linda came into Bassets in the early 1970's and showed for a while but found hunting much more interesting. Peter whipped-in to the Albany Bassets (now Albany & West Lodge) for many years, and Linda has acted as Field Master. Peter currently runs the Limited Odds Draw, which raises funds for the pack. Their son Mark is Senior Master and amateur Huntsman of the British East Lincs. Bassets.

See Chapter Two: "Hunting With Basset Hounds".

ROSEMARY IZARD CORBETT (MOONSMEAD)

Rosemary grew up in a Basset household. "I was given a thorough grounding in 'Bassetology', mainly by the doyennes of the breed during that time – my mother (Joan Izard), Mildred Seiffert, Anne Mathews, Veronica Ross and Peg Walton," says Rosemary. "I went to work in Mildred Seiffert's famous Maycombe Kennel. Here I was entrusted with the care of her beautiful hounds – Ancestor, Polygamy, Jemima, Flaxen and many others; this gave me an excellent insight into show Bassets. At that time Mildred Seiffert imported several dogs from Peg Walton (USA). Lyn Mar Acres Endman became my absolute 'pin up'. I searched through the *Tally Ho* magazine for photographs of him, and, during this search, became intrigued by the tracking hounds who were always featured in the magazines and yearbooks.

"A lifelong friend of my mother's, Peg was a frequent visitor to the UK. I became very interested in tracking, which had become a popular hobby in the States. At the time there was little reference to training hounds to track, and it was not until I imported my own American hounds (20 years later) from Mr & Mrs R Fredericksen, that I got the chance to learn. Tracking with Bassets has been a personal interest for over 30 years; I feel it is quite important to keep the Basset Hound's purpose/working abilty alive and I am happy to help others who are interested in this absorbing pastime.

See Chapter Six: "Tracking Tips".

JULIA BARNES

Julia has owned and trained a number of different dog breeds, and has also worked as a puppy socialiser for Dogs for the Disabled. A former journalist, she has written many books, including several on dog training and behaviour. Julia is indebted to the editors for their specialist knowledge about Bassets.

See Chapter Six: Socialisation and Training.

ALISON LOGAN MA VetMB MRCVS

Alison qualified as a veterinary surgeon from Cambridge University in 1989, having been brought up surrounded by all manner of animals and birds in the north Essex countryside. She has been in practice in her home town ever since, living with her husband, two children and Labrador Retriever Pippin.

She contributes on a regular basis to *Veterinary Times, Veterinary Nurse Times, Dogs Today, Cat World* and *Pet Patter*, the PetPlan newsletter. In 1995, Alison won the Univet Literary Award with an article on Cushing's Disease, and she won it again (as the Vetoquinol Literary Award) in 2002, writing about common conditions in the Shar-Pei.

See Chapter Eight: Happy and Healthy.

MARCY ZINGLER (US CONSULTANT)

Marcy L. Zingler was Senior Editor at Howell Book House before joining the AKC staff as Corporate Project Manager. One of her primary responsibilities was as Project Editor for the award-winning AKC 125th Anniversary book. As a freelancer, she was the only outside editor to work on *The AKC Complete Dog Book*, 20th Edition and 19th Revised.

Marcy's 40-year participation in the dog sport has included breeding, exhibiting, judging, and active leadership in national clubs as officeholder, AKC Delegate and Judges' Education Chair. A three-time National Specialty judge in her original breed, she has judged across the US and in Australia.

Now semi-retired, she again serves as a Delegate to the American Kennel Club.

COL. ROBERT E. BOOTH (USAF, RET.) AMERICA

Robert E. (Bob) Booth has been breeding and showing Basset Hounds under the Hiflite prefix since the early 1960s. A dog bred by him became Top Sire in the breed's history with 67 champion get.

Bob has been a conformation judge of Bassets since 1971, and has had the honor of judging the Basset Hound Club of America (BHCA) Annual National Specialty Show on four different occasions. He judges the entire Hound Group and the majority of the Non-Sporting Group.

He is the author of The Official Book of the Basset Hound and was awarded life membership in the BHCA. Bob is now retired as a Colonel in the U.S. Air Force where he was a pilot for nearly 26 years. He resides with his wife, Sandra, in the Texas hill country.

ANN CARIUS (AARU, AUSTRALIA)

Ann purchased her first Basset in 1970. Ralph's pedigree was predominantly English featuring ancestors from the Grims, Carillon and Skyemoor kennels. He was exhibited briefly. In the ensuing years the Aaru kennels have produced only eight litters but have enjoyed success at All Breeds and Specialty shows. The Kortebin imports have each been Specialty winners.

Ann's daughter Ainslee shares her love of the breed and has handled Bassets for many Australian kennels. She is also an accredited Hound Judge.

Ann has been a member of the Basset Hound Club of Queensland since its inception and was the club's President for many years. Ainslee is the President of Dogs Queensland and was formerly Secretary of the Queensland Basset Hound Club .

DALE WILKINSON (BASSETDALE, NEW ZEALAND)

The Bassetdale Kennels of New Zealand were first registered in 1967 by Sue and Dale Wilkinson. Their first dog was Ch. Baronne De Jayville, sired by Ch. Grimms Wawcott, dam Suffolk Cindy Out of Grims Caroline.

The Kennel enjoyed considerable success, being the top-winning Basset Kennel in New Zealand and having owned the top-winning Basset NZ Grand Ch. Sagaces Little Richard (imported Australia) and the top-wnning bitch Ch. Courtside Utah Stars. Dale has also judged the breed throughout the world, though he and Sue are now largely retired, showing only to maintain their interest in the breed that they love.

GRACE SERVAIS (NEW BELLECOMBE, SWITZERLAND)

Grace Servais has lived in Switzerland for a number of years showing dogs under the Bellecombe affix.

"In 1978, my husband said 'I've seen the breed of dog I'd like to have: a Hush Puppy! Why don't we get one?' My answer was: 'Well, why not?'. Neither of us had seen one in Switzerland, but had seen one with Lieutenant Columbo in the American crime series on TV; we found the Basset's tragi-comic expression and individualistic nature most appealing. I was delegated to find and buy our first Basset. I bought Maycombe Danseuse (Sally), by telephone, from well-known British breeder, Mrs Mildred Seiffert (Maycombe) – who later became my close friend and mentor. I brought Sally home on Christmas Eve.

"Mildred put me in touch with an English Basset breeder/exhibitor residing in Switzerland who introduced me to the Basset and Bloodhound Club der Schweiz (BBCS), which I joined. At the next BBCS Club Show, Sally went 3rd Excellent in a class of 10 and I was hooked! Several shows later, Sally having won a couple of CACIBs and RCACIBs, I thought about breeding Bassets. I applied for, and obtained, the affix Bellecombe.

"Sally failed to produce puppies so I imported another bitch (Galants Emily) from England. In Switzerland, all puppies of a litter must have the 'calling name' beginning with the same letter. My 'A' litter (Galants Emily x Ch. Lonesome Lover v. Hollandheim) was born in February, 1984. I kept Araminta. So far, I have bred 20 litters. Two very promising puppies (Troy and Tuppence) from the T litter (Multi-Ch. Bellecombe No no Nanette x Multi Ch. Davinci v. Hollandheim), born on 1st July, 2010, will remain with me. Clearly the Bellecombe kennel has a history of breeding for quality rather than quantity!

"In 2008, my daughter, Jackie Beare, became the kennel co-owner and the name was changed to New Bellecombe: an affix protected by the Fédération Cynologique Internationale (FCI). Starting with the S litter (Multi Ch. Bellecombe No no Nanette x Ch. Aramis du Jardin d'Esméralda), all our puppies carry the affix. So much for our beginnings. Suffice it to say that New Bellecombe is still going strong!

USEFUL ADDRESSES

KENNEL & BREED CLUBS

UK
The Kennel Club
1 Clarges Street, London, W1J 8AB
Tel: 0870 606 6750
Fax: 0207 518 1058
Web: www.the-kennel-club.org.uk

To obtain up-to-date contact information for the following breed clubs, contact the Kennel Club:
- Basset Hound Club (national organisation with regional divisions)
- Basset Hound Club Of Northern Ireland
- Basset Hound Club of Scotland
- Basset Hound Club of Wales
- Hadrian Basset Hound Club
- Lancashire, Yorkshire & Cheshire Basset Hound Club
- Midland Basset Hound Club
- South of England Basset Hound Club

USA
American Kennel Club (AKC)
5580 Centerview Drive,
Raleigh, NC 27606, USA.
Tel: 919 233 9767
Fax: 919 233 3627
Email: info@akc.org
Web: www.akc.org

United Kennel Club (UKC)
100 E Kilgore Rd, Kalamazoo,
MI 49002-5584, USA.
Tel: 269 343 9020
Fax: 269 343 7037
Web:www.ukcdogs.com/

Basset Hound Club of America, Inc
Web: http://basset-bhca.com/

For contact details of regional clubs, please contact the Basset Hound Club of America.

AUSTRALIA & NEW ZEALAND
Australian National Kennel Council (ANKC)
The Australian National Kennel Council is the administrative body for pure breed canine affairs in Australia. It does not, however, deal directly with dog exhibitors, breeders or judges. For information pertaining to breeders, clubs or shows, please contact the relevant State or Territory Controlling Body.

Dogs Australian Capital Territory
PO Box 815, Dickson ACT 2602
Tel: (02) 6241 4404
Fax: (02) 6241 1129
Email: administrator@dogsact.org.au
Web: www.dogsact.org.au

Dogs New South Wales
PO Box 632, St Marys, NSW 1790
Tel: (02) 9834 3022 or 1300 728 022 (NSW Only)
Fax: (02) 9834 3872

Email: info@dogsnsw.org.au
Web: www.dogsnsw.org.au

Dogs Northern Territory
PO Box 37521, Winnellie NT 0821
Tel: (08) 8984 3570
Fax: (08) 8984 3409
Email: admin@dogsnt.com.au
Web: www.dogsnt.com.au

Dogs Queensland
PO Box 495, Fortitude Valley Qld 4006
Tel: (07) 3252 2661
Fax: (07) 3252 3864
Email: info@dogsqueensland.org.au
Web: www.dogsqueensland.org.au

Dogs South Australia
PO Box 844
Prospect East SA 5082
Tel: (08) 8349 4797
Fax: (08) 8262 5751
Email: info@dogssa.com.au
Web: www.dogssa.com.au

Tasmanian Canine Association Inc
The Rothman Building,
PO Box 116
Glenorchy Tas 7010
Tel: (03) 6272 9443
Fax: (03) 6273 0844
Email: tca@iprimus.com.au
Web: www.tasdogs.com

Dogs Victoria
Locked Bag K9
Cranbourne VIC 3977
Tel: (03)9788 2500
Fax: (03) 9788 2599
Email: office@dogsvictoria.org.au
Web: www.dogsvictoria.org.au

Dogs Western Australia
PO Box 1404
Canning Vale WA 6970
Tel: (08) 9455 1188
Fax: (08) 9455 1190
Email: k9@dogswest.com
Web: www.dogswest.com

New Zealand Kennel Club
Prosser Street, Private Bag 50903,
Porirua 5240, NZ.
Tel: (04) 237 4489
Fax: (04) 237 0721
Web: www.nzkc.org.nz

INTERNATIONAL
Fédération Cynologique Internationalé (FCI)/World Canine Organisation
Place Albert 1er, 13, B-6530 Thuin,
Belgium.
Tel: +32 71 59.12.38
Fax: +32 71 59.22.29
Web: www.fci.be/

TRAINING AND BEHAVIOUR

UK
Association of Pet Dog Trainers
PO Box 17, Kempsford, GL7 4WZ
Telephone: 01285 810811
Email: APDToffice@aol.com
Web: http://www.apdt.co.uk

Association of Pet Behaviour Counsellors
PO BOX 46, Worcester, WR8 9YS
Telephone: 01386 751151
Fax: 01386 750743
Email: info@apbc.org.uk
Web: http://www.apbc.org.uk/

USA
Association of Pet Dog Trainers
101 North Main Street, Suite 610
Greenville, SC 29601, USA.
Tel: 1 800 738 3647
Email: information@apdt.com
Web: www.apdt.com/

American College of Veterinary Behaviorists
College of Veterinary Medicine, 4474 Tamu,
Texas A&M University
College Station, Texas 77843-4474
Web: http://dacvb.org/

American Veterinary Society of Animal Behavior
Web: www.avsabonline.org/

AUSTRALIA
APDT Australia Inc
PO Box 3122, Bankstown Square, NSW 2200,
Email: secretary@apdt.com.au
Web: www.apdt.com.au

Canine Behaviour
For details of regional behvaiourists, contact the relevant State or Territory Controlling Body.

ACTIVITIES

UK
Agility Club
http://www.agilityclub.co.uk/

British Flyball Association
PO Box 990, Doncaster, DN1 9FY
Telephone: 01628 829623
Email: secretary@flyball.org.uk
Web: http://www.flyball.org.uk/

USA
North American Dog Agility Council
P.O. Box 1206, Colbert,
OK 74733, USA.
Web: www.nadac.com/

North American Flyball Association, Inc.
1333 West Devon Avenue, #512

Chicago, IL 60660
Tel/Fax: 800 318 6312
Email: flyball@flyball.org
Web: www.flyball.org/

AUSTRALIA
Agility Dog Association of Australia
ADAA Secretary, PO Box 2212,
Gailes, QLD 4300, Australia.
Tel: 0423 138 914
Email: admin@adaa.com.au
Web: www.adaa.com.au/

NADAC Australia (North American Dog Agility Council - Australian Division)
12 Wellman Street, Box Hill South, Victoria 3128, Australia.
Email: shirlene@nadacaustralia.com
Web: www.nadacaustralia.com/

Australian Flyball Association
PO Box 4179, Pitt Town, NSW 2756
Tel: 0407 337 939
Email: info@flyball.org.au
Web: www.flyball.org.au/

INTERNATIONAL
World Canine Freestyle Organisation
P.O. Box 350122, Brooklyn, NY 11235-2525, USA
Tel: (718) 332-8336
Fax: (718) 646-2686
Email: wcfodogs@aol.com
Web: www.worldcaninefreestyle.org

HEALTH

UK
Alternative Veterinary Medicine Centre
Chinham House, Stanford in the Vale,
Oxfordshire, SN7 8NQ
Tel: 01367 710324
Fax: 01367 718243
Web: www.alternativevet.org/

British Small Animal Veterinary Association
Woodrow House, 1 Telford Way,
Waterwells Business Park, Quedgeley,
Gloucestershire, GL2 2AB
Tel: 01452 726700
Fax: 01452 726701
Email: customerservices@bsava.com
Web: http://www.bsava.com/

Royal College of Veterinary Surgeons
Belgravia House, 62-64 Horseferry Road,
London, SW1P 2AF
Tel: 0207 222 2001
Fax: 0207 222 2004
Email: admin@rcvs.org.uk
Web: www.rcvs.org.uk

USA
American Holistic Veterinary Medical Association
2218 Old Emmorton Road
Bel Air, MD 21015
Tel: 410 569 0795
Fax 410 569 2346
Email: office@ahvma.org
Web: www.ahvma.org/

American Veterinary Medical Association
1931 North Meacham Road, Suite 100,
Schaumburg, IL 60173-4360, USA.
Tel: 800 248 2862
Fax: 847 925 1329
Web: www.avma.org

American College of Veterinary Surgeons
19785 Crystal Rock Dr, Suite 305
Germantown, MD 20874, USA.
Tel: 301 916 0200
Toll Free: 877 217 2287
Fax: 301 916 2287
Email: acvs@acvs.org
Web: www.acvs.org/

AUSTRALIA
Australian Holistic Vets
Web: www.ahv.com.au/

Australian Small Animal Veterinary Association
40/6 Herbert Street, St Leonards, NSW 2065,
Australia.
Tel: 02 9431 5090
Fax: 02 9437 9068
Email: asava@ava.com.au
Web: www.asava.com.au

Australian Veterinary Association
Unit 40, 6 Herbert Street, St Leonards, NSW
2065, Australia.
Tel: 02 9431 5000
Fax: 02 9437 9068
Web: www.ava.com.au

Australian College Veterinary Scientists
Building 3, Garden City Office Park,
2404 Logan Road, Eight Mile Plains,
Queensland 4113, Australia.
Tel: 07 3423 2016
Fax: 07 3423 2977
Email: admin@acvs.org.au
Web: http://acvsc.org.au

ASSISTANCE DOGS

UK
Canine Partners
Mill Lane, Heyshott, Midhurst, GU29 0ED
Tel: 08456 580480
Fax: 08456 580481
Web: www.caninepartners.co.uk

Dogs for the Disabled
The Frances Hay Centre, Blacklocks Hill,
Banbury, Oxon, OX17 2BS
Tel: 01295 252600
Web: www.dogsforthedisabled.org

Guide Dogs for the Blind Association
Burghfield Common, Reading, RG7 3YG
Tel: 01189 835555
Fax: 01189 835433
Web: www.guidedogs.org.uk/
Hearing Dogs for Deaf People
The Grange, Wycombe Road, Saunderton,
Princes Risborough, Bucks, HP27 9NS
Tel: 01844 348100
Fax: 01844 348101
Web: www.hearingdogs.org.uk

Pets as Therapy
14a High Street, Wendover, Aylesbury, Bucks.
HP22 6EA.
Tel: 01845 345445
Fax: 01845 550236
Web: http://www.petsastherapy.org/

Support Dogs
21 Jessops Riverside, Brightside Lane, Sheffield,
S9 2RX
Tel: 01142 617800
Fax: 01142 617555
Email: supportdogs@btconnect.com
Web: www.support-dogs.org.uk

USA
Therapy Dogs International
88 Bartley Road, Flanders, NJ 07836,.
Tel: 973 252 9800
Fax: 973 252 7171
Web: www.tdi-dog.o

Therapy Dogs Inc.
P.O. Box 20227, Cheyenne, WY 82003.
Tel: 307 432 0272.
Fax: 307-638-2079
Web: www.therapydogs.com

Delta Society - Pet Partners
875 124th Ave NE, Suite 101 • Bellevue, WA
98005 USA.
Email: info@DeltaSociety.org
Web: www.deltasociety.org

Comfort Caring Canines
8135 Lare Street, Philadelphia, PA 19128.
Email: ccc@comfortcaringcanines.org
Web: www.comfortcaringcanines.org/

AUSTRALIA
AWARE Dogs Australia, Inc
PO Box 883, Kuranda, Queensland, 488..
Tel: 07 4093 8152
Web: www.awaredogs.org.au/

Delta Society -- Therapy Dogs
Web: www.deltasociety.com.au